THE JESUS LETTERS

SEVEN SECRETS THAT CAN *change* YOU AND YOUR CHURCH

DAVID RAVENHILL

Destiny Image® Publishers, Inc.
P.O. Box 310
Shippensburg, PA 17257-0310

"Speaking to the Purposes of God for This Generation
and for the Generations to Come"

ISBN 0-7684-2173-X

For Worldwide Distribution
Printed in the U.S.A.

This book and all other Destiny Image, Revival Press,
MercyPlace, Fresh Bread, Destiny Image Fiction,
and Treasure House books are available
at Christian bookstores and distributors worldwide.

For a U.S. bookstore nearest you, call **1-800-722-6774**.
For more information on foreign distributors, call **717-532-3040**.
Or reach us on the Internet:
www.destinyimage.com

DEDICATION

To the Lord Jesus Christ

My changeless Father
My majestic King
My incredible Master
My sovereign Savior
My merciful High Priest
My tireless Intercessor
My faithful Shepherd
My loyal Defender
My abundant Provider
My ultimate Judge
My Life Giver
My living Word
My best Friend

ACKNOWLEDGMENTS

I want to thank all those who assisted me with the completion of this my third book.

David Hazzard for his outstanding work in editing. He is considered by many to be one of the best in the business. I agree.

Micki Milam for the many hours of transcribing my manuscript from longhand to type.

The Destiny Image staff, who provided both encouragement and the cooperation necessary to bring this to completion.

The many friends who have faithfully upheld me in prayer and continue to pray for my ministry.

My wonderful wife, Nancy, for her tireless love and support, without which I could not make it.

To each and every one of you my deep and sincere thanks.

ENDORSEMENTS

"How refreshing! Something besides junk mail! In *The Jesus Letters*, David Ravenhill has done it again. With the heart of a pastor and the fire of an evangelist, he expounds on the Word of God and challenges us all. Here's a writer who leaves no stone unturned. Thanks, David! Reader...you've got mail."

—Stephen L. Hill
Evangelist

"I picked up this book with great anticipation and I was not disappointed. This is David Ravenhill at his best: a seasoned man of God pointing us to Jesus alone, jarring us with divine reality, sobering us with scriptural truth, challenging us to evaluate our lives and ministries afresh in the light of God's unchanging Word. I highly recommend this penetrating and practical exposition of Revelation 1–3. Read it and be changed!"

—Dr. Michael L. Brown,
President, FIRE School of Ministry

"From the vantage point of almost 40 years in ministry, David Ravenhill issues a fresh challenge to the Church to fulfill its destiny in this urgent hour. 9-11 was a wake-up call for the Church but, as it's been said, many have pressed the snooze alarm and gone back to sleep. This book will stir us out of any slumber, so that we will see a glorious Church in these glorious days that are before us. This book can change your life!"

—Larry Tomczak
Senior Pastor at Christ the King Church, Epistolic leader
Author of *Reckless Abandon* and *Divine Appointments*

CONTENTS

INTRODUCTION

THE STORY IS TOLD OF A YOUNG SOLDIER who was walking through a graveyard when he came across a headstone that caught his eye. On it was inscribed this epitaph:

Remember, friend, as you pass by

As now you are, so once was I.

As now I am, soon you will be.

Prepare for death and follow me.

As the soldier pondered these words, he walked away wishing he could add this concluding thought:

To follow thee I'm not content,

Until I know which way you went.

We would do well, today, to apply this bit of wisdom to those who lead us in this world—most especially, I believe, to our spiritual leaders. Do we really know, when we submit our lives to the teaching, guidance, and direction of a spiritual leader, where exactly he or she is leading us?

Leadership by its very nature is founded on the idea that the leader knows where he is going. The apostle Paul was most definite about his own direction, and where he was leading those souls in his charge when he said "Be imitators of me, just as I also am of Christ" (1 Cor. 11:1). As Paul was called by the living Christ whom he followed, so he in turn called others to follow him in his lifelong pursuit of the Holy One, the Lord of all who live.

Things have not changed from Paul's day until now in the Kingdom of God. As Christians, we are still called—everyone of us—to follow Christ, the risen Lord. To clear up any confusion from the beginning, let me say quickly that to follow Christ is to agree with Him and live according to the standards He has given us to follow. Herein lies the Church's problem in every age. We agree that Jesus is the Lord; we don't agree with what He has told us to do—not in the full, true sense that matters, which is to agree with Him by living and doing what He has told us to do.

Lest you think this is going to become another diatribe about "sin" in our personal lives I can assure you I am going at the root of an even deeper problem—one that affects us, not just as individuals, but as a whole body of believers. What is the problem here? For far too long the Church has evaluated its progress, not according to the standards Christ has set for us, but according to the world's standards.

When we live by any other standard than the one Christ has asked us to follow we inevitably find that we've strayed into a spiritually barren and rocky place. We say we're "dry," "bored," "feeling lifeless," "lacking direction." We say we need " a fresh visitation."

As I travel to churches throughout the world, it seems clear we need to face these needs now. And more than that, we need to face the more basic problem that is causing these conditions.

WHOSE STANDARD ARE WE FOLLOWING?

The purpose of this book is to reveal how the head of the Church, the Lord Jesus Christ, calls His Church out of soul-distressing places where we have wandered on our own, and calls us back to vibrant, powerful life in His Spirit. He has never left us on our own, without a path on which to follow Him in the eternal, ever-new kind of life He offers us. It is we who have gone astray, and turned to our own ways.

The purpose of this book is to call us—the leaders of God's flock, and everyone in the flock—back into the ways in which God has clearly called us to walk. It is only after we understand His ways that we can truly follow Him. And only as we follow Him can we please Him. I believe it was A.W. Tozer who said, "The Christian life can be reduced down to this basic teaching. Learn to love what God loves and hate what God hates."

"HEAR WHAT THE SPIRIT IS SAYING TO THE CHURCHES..."

In the Book of Revelation we have a clear and succinct series of statements from the Lord Jesus Christ about what He loves and what He hates. He leaves nothing to guesswork. He tells us what brings the reward of His presence and pleasure and what brings the punishment of His absence from us and coldness of spirit that signals His displeasure. Since He speaks clearly here, we would do well to pay careful attention if we want to live as His true followers in His Church.

The statements I'm referring to are, of course, found in the first three chapters of Revelation, in the letters that our Lord "dictated" to the visionary apostle John. They are addressed to the seven churches in Asia Minor, and they refer to spiritual maladies that are leading the churches offtrack. Within these letters, the Lord Himself reveals the root causes of the various spiritual maladies that are keeping His churches from following Him in the way He desires. And while the diagnoses sting, the medicine He gives has a wonderfully restorative quality.

MEDICINE FOR THE WHOLE CHURCH

My belief is that these letters apply not only to the churches in Asia Minor to whom they are addressed, but also to the whole Church for all time. For in them we find the Lord clearly speaking of symptoms of spiritual ailments—misunderstanding, sins, laxities, failings, even heretical teachings—which seem always to have plagued the Body of Christ, and which still plague the Church today. Moreover, the spiritual "medicines" we find recommended in these letters are as good for us today as they were for churches in Asia Minor those many centuries ago. Best of all, the diagnoses and directions that the Lord Jesus Christ gives to them are full of divine insight, and also promise that spiritual strength, vision, passion, and health will be restored.

As we explore together these seven letters to the churches, recorded in Revelation, we will gain insight into what Christ asks of us. We will understand the rewards in practical godly living and in spirit that will be ours if we follow the ways of our divine Lord and Master. We can be sure of these rewards because the words of Christ to His churches are timeless. They come from the living Word and so they are still potent, active, and life-giving today...for those who have ears to hear.

May every Christian leader and follower hear what the Spirit is still saying to the churches.

CHAPTER 1

THE BIG QUESTION

FOR A NUMBER OF YEARS I've had the privilege of traveling extensively throughout the United States and all across the world, teaching and preaching in gatherings that number from a few to sometimes thousands. I've spoken at colleges, conferences, and in many local churches.

At some time during the course of my stay I'm asked the question, "Brother Ravenhill, what do you hear God saying to the Church?" or "What do you see happening as you travel? What is God doing?"

THE REAL QUESTION

Behind the question, for some, there is a deep cry to understand the will of God for their own life and for the life of the congregation entrusted to their leadership. They really want to know how to please God. For others, the motivation seems to be some other impulse—a sort of desire to "keep up with the Joneses." They usually make it clear they just want to know what techniques, programs, or trends are "working" elsewhere. And by "working" they usually mean, "What's bringing in a crowd?"

or "What's keeping people pumped up with zeal and energy?" The size of the crowd, and the amount of noise and energy, seem to be the "sacred" standards of measure too many leaders and their flocks go by, judging themselves to be healthy or unhealthy based on body count and decibel level, I presume.

Given the many times I've encountered this question over the years, I've longed for a godly reply to offer in both situations—one that solidly, clearly reflects the mind of the Lord. But I have also found myself somewhat dismayed.

What is truly disconcerting to me is that the ones who are asking the questions—"What is God saying? What is God doing?"—are the very ones that congregations are looking to for spiritual insight and direction. How disillusioned would many of us be, to discover that our leader is just as confused and wandering spiritually as we are?

Putting this in the context of the New Testament, some who are asking this question may be among those who are classified as "blind leaders of the blind" (see Mt. 15:14). I hasten to say that I am not speaking with disdain or superiority; God forbid. Rather, I'm making the point that there is a great need in this hour for the Church to hear again the directing voice of the Spirit; in fact, an acute need.

A FAMINE OF HEARING

I say the need is acute, for we seem to be in a time period like the one spoken of by the prophet Amos over two millennia ago: " 'Behold, days are coming,' declares the Lord God, 'when I will send a famine on the land, not a famine for bread or a thirst for water, but rather for *hearing* the words of the Lord' " (Amos 8:11).

It is important to notice what Amos does not say. He doesn't speak of a famine of God's Word. Amos warns about a coming famine of *hearing*.

Never before in history have we had more translations of the Bible than we do now. As for Christian books, they are as numerous as the stars of Heaven—everything from diets to demons, health to holiness, prosperity to prophecy, and all subjects in between. And yet our greatest need is not to hear opinions, but to hear the Word of the Lord.

This need is especially acute for those in spiritual leadership, because we are not only supposed to be acting in the name of the Lord, but in accordance with His will, in our work for Him. All of us will one day give an account of our works.

WHOSE CHURCH ARE WE BUILDING?

As Paul admonished the church in Corinth, "Take heed how you build" (see 1 Cor. 3:10). He then explained the urgency of the need—because "the day...will test the quality of each man's work" (1 Cor. 3:13b).

The Bible makes it abundantly clear that those in spiritual leadership will receive the greater judgment concerning their works. "From everyone who has been given much, much will be required" (Lk. 12:48b). James states it best when he writes, "Let not many of you become teachers, my brethren, knowing that as such we will incur a stricter judgment" (Jas. 3:1).

We, the leaders of God's flock, desperately need ears to hear what the Spirit is saying to the Church. For it is not *our* Church we are building, but His.

Sadly, though, we often look to sources other than the Lord, when it comes to this business of "building the church." Many of us turn to large conferences or seminars to find "the latest blueprint." And many times we're offered, as our example, someone who has a "successful ministry." We're to assume that they have the answers to the Church's need. This is implied, supposedly, by the measure of success they've achieved, and usually this success is measured by the size of their congregation or the listening audience of their radio or television ministry. For some, their success is measured by the sales of their latest book, the one that's just taken the Christian world by storm.

But is success in the Kingdom of God measured by size and sales? If size is our standard, we might as well consider merging our churches with the Mormon church, with its rapidly expanding empires, or with some new age cult that is capturing the hearts of people as it spreads like a virus across the land.

Though it is certainly not true of all men who grow large churches or whose books become bestsellers, many leaders have proved only that they know how to succeed in numbers and popularity. What we don't know is whether they've succeeded by the Lord's standard or by some other—such as by delivering what a great number of people want to hear.

Tragically, as we've seen, some of these "superstar" careers are short-lived. Their man-made empires come crashing down around them due to moral failure or burnout. My friend Mike Bickle defines burnout as trying to walk in another man's calling or anointing. Others achieve a following among leaders who flock to their churches to study what they've done. These teachers then return to their home churches where they try to duplicate the "success" in their locale—only to get dismal results.

The question then becomes: How tuned in to the mind and will of the Lord were these leaders? Or for that matter, how in tuned to the mind and will of the Lord were the people who followed them?

We should be asking ourselves: Are too many leaders merely great communicators and creative administrators who know how to build quickly something which cannot stand when the rains descend and the floods come? And on what standard do we base success in building for the Lord?

CHARACTER FIRST

If we are going to build in the Kingdom of God, it is first and foremost imperative that we emphasize spiritual character over charisma. Spiritual character is not determined by the brilliance of our so-called gifts, or our ability to communicate, or our ability to draw up "blueprints for growth," or to administrate. With these we can build our own churches and ministries, and they can be very large indeed.

Spiritual character is determined by our ability to hear and closely follow what the Lord is telling us to do as He builds His Church.

The question, I repeat, is: Whose church are we building?

If it is the Lord's Church, it behooves us to listen carefully. For we need to hear clearly what the Spirit of the Lord is saying to His Church.

Chapter 2

Is Anyone Listening?

Suppose a world-famous botanist wanted to study the exotic plants of the South American rain forest. Where do you think the best place to begin would be? Obviously, in the rain forest itself.

Why is it then, when we want to determine the will of God for the Church, we so often turn to sources other than God Himself?

Part of my daily ritual, when I am not traveling, is to check my e-mail, an incredible twentieth-century invention that is both a blessing and a curse. I am staggered at the abundance of "prophetic words" I receive weekly. These prophecies concern everything from what God is saying concerning some city or nation, to predicting who the next president of the United States will be. I finally had to ask to be removed from one list because I do not have the time to pore over these "words from God." Don't misunderstand, I'm not despising prophecy. But I have to wonder how much time these people spend alone with God, especially because I'm not acquainted with them yet their prophecies seem to pour forth like Niagara.

THE SURE WORD

I believe it is time for the Church to return to the more sure word of prophecy—the Word of God itself. The true gift of prophecy has enormous value, make no mistake. But it is my belief that we first sharpen our spiritual listening abilities by learning how to get tuned in to what the Spirit has already said to us—the whole Church, for all time—through the Scriptures.

Most Evangelicals and Pentecostals readily accept the Bible as God's divinely inspired Word. For instance, if you asked most Christians about the great doctrine of the atonement they would immediately turn to the appropriate passages dealing with this glorious truth. Or if we wished to understand something concerning marriage or spiritual warfare, once again, we would know where to read. We believe God's Word in Scripture to be timeless.

Imagine, then, that you have just asked someone about tithing and they respond, "Well, two thousand years ago, Paul said such and such. But I'm not quite sure what God is saying about that today." You would immediately recognize that this person was either ignorant or deceived. Why? Because we understand that God's Word is both fixed and firm—and it is living and active, as well. This means, what was true two thousand years ago is still applicable for today.

God's Word has both a past and yes, a current prophetic application.

WHAT THE SPIRIT HAS ALWAYS BEEN SAYING

Unfortunately, here is where many of us go astray. When it comes to understanding the mind of God concerning the present-day Church, we don't necessarily want to know what's already been said. That can seem like old news. Nothing exciting there.

So when we hear the Lord's admonition to us in Revelation—"He that hath ears to hear, let him hear what the Spirit says to the Church"—we do a bit of modification. We don't modify the wording of His directive, but we change the intent. We do so by lifting this admonition out all by itself, thereby not directing our full attention to the seven letters that come after it.

When we do this, we set out after *new* and *current revelations*, while missing foundational commands and correctives already given to us by the Lord. I would go so far as to say that by seeking new and "fresh" revelations, we sometimes choose to ignore what has already been revealed to us by the Word of God.

When we ignore what the Spirit has said that applies for all time, we do so at great peril.

A BLIND LEAP

I must confess that for years, I was very eager to hear the "fresh" words of God. If only I could have ears to hear God's current message to the Church! I had taken a blind leap of faith from the foundation of God's Word in Scripture because I desperately wanted to hear His message for the Church today. Of course I didn't think this way on issues that Jesus talked about; to do so would have been an act of heresy.

Only in recent years have I realized how easy it is to stray from the ways of God when you seek "fresh" revelation while ignoring what is foundational to the Church in the eternal Word.

Some years ago on the West Coast, a group of churches experienced a wonderful move of God's Spirit. This group had been founded by a man who had experienced deep insights in his private times with the Lord. They eventually grew to become a network of churches, including many overseas. However, the leader became "convinced" that it was all right for him to leave his wife for another woman, and used a whole line of convoluted reasoning that led him to declare he was being given permission by God to do this "for the sake of the Kingdom of God." It was easy to see through this "fresh revelation" and recognize that this was merely an excuse to marry another woman whom he thought would be "a better asset" to his ministry. Very quickly, his grave error led others to imitate his example, and immorality followed.

Whether our failures are big and public, or private and before the Lord, we will fail if we do not hear and heed the foundational commands He has given to His Church. Our failure may not be visible and media-worthy—but still we will have failed to follow Christ.

Perhaps what we needed is not so much a fresh word, as a fresh "burden."

Increasingly, I have witnessed our need as the people of God to study and know the Word of God as it was delivered to the early Church by Christ Himself in its formative days. I have been burdened by a need to study God's Word to the Church, as set forth in the first three chapters of Revelation. Why? Because I recognize that it is not only applicable but also essential to the Church today.

What I am suggesting is that our hearts need to be burdened with the carrying out of the will of Christ for His Church. This is what we find, so clearly stated, in the first three chapters of Revelation.

"TO THE SEVEN CHURCHES...WRITE THIS..."

The Word of God that is given to the Church is set forth in letters to "seven churches" (see Rev. 1–3). Of course there were more than seven Christian congregations in existence at that time. So what is the significance of the Lord's addressing "seven churches"?

When we read the Book of Revelation it becomes apparent very quickly that it abounds with "sevens." First come the seven letters to seven churches, giving them prominence and priority. But there are also seven seals and seven trumpets. Seven vials and seven Spirits. Seven angels, seven plagues, seven lamps. The list goes on. It's clear that something more than numeric value is being expressed. In fact, *seven* represents the concept of unity, completeness, or fullness.

That the Word of God is being given to seven churches tells us that God is revealing His heart and mind to His universal Church. And what He has to say goes far beyond the scope of the individual churches to which each letter is addressed. And yet, there has been a tendency to read these letters as if we were sneaking a look in someone else's mail. Those problems that the Lord addressed...and those directives...well, aren't they specifically intended for those people back then?

Oddly enough, we have readily accepted Paul's writings to the Corinthians, Ephesians, Colossians, and other churches as inspired and applicable to the Church today. We look far beyond the historic application and eagerly embrace them as God's timeless message to His people no matter what generation they live in. Once again it's clear: We cannot contemporize the Lord's command—"Hear what the Spirit is saying to the churches"—and then skip over the actual messages that follow.

WILL WE BE FOUND FAITHFUL?

I trust that you are beginning to see how seriously we have erred by de-emphasizing or ignoring the universal and eternal messages to the seven churches, while pursuing current "words."

The message from the Lord Jesus Christ, as contained in these first three chapters of Revelation, is of utmost importance to us today. We dare not overlook it, for it is God's timeless instruction to His Church.

If we are the Church, we will pay careful attention, for it is by these standards that we will be measured. And we will either be found to be wandering in our own way, seeking success in our own eyes and the eyes of the world...or we will be found walking faithfully in the ways of God.

CHAPTER 3

THE CALLED-OUT ONES

BEFORE WE EXPLORE THE LORD'S MESSAGE to His Church, it's of utmost importance that we define what we mean by "the Church."

For many leaders today, and their flocks, "the Church" means *this* church—the one I worship in every Sunday. For others who have established fellowship with other congregations nearby, it means the church *in this area*. Those who have denominational or other affiliations may refer to the church *in our group*. Beyond that, we have only a vague sense of the Church universal.

What I am trying to show you is that most of us have this uncanny ability to reduce the Church. We whittle it down, as it were, until amazingly, we and those who think just like us are the ones standing at the center of it.

AMERICA—A NOT-SO-GOOD EXAMPLE

Some years ago there was a popular movie entitled *Honey, I Shrunk the Kids*. Although I never saw the film, the title alone tells the story. Normal-sized children suddenly find themselves turned into miniatures.

What was merely Hollywood fantasy, unfortunately, has become reality when applied to our understanding of the Church. I say this because I have found that the average Christian leader, as well the average believer, has very little understanding of the Church or her role. Perhaps other Christians, viewing the state of the Church from the countries in which they live would say the same thing, but I find this tendency to misunderstand and reduce the Church is especially true in the United States.

Not long ago, for instance, America went through a hotly-contended presidential election. The outcome of this election was certainly very important, make no mistake. But as I listened to the prayers that were offered, asking God to resolve the tensions following history's closest political contest, I perceived a major blind spot in American believers' view of the Church. In short, I could have sworn that the Church had been replaced by "America." The gist of the prayers were for God to spare this great nation that was to play such an important role in God's purpose. It seemed that without the United States, God was in serious trouble. What was God going to do if He lost the only vessel He had?

Now you might think I'm just a bitter, British "bloke," holding a personal grudge against America for separating from Britain. Not so. I claim America as my home, having immigrated here with my parents decades ago when I was 14. I love this country. I'm married to an American, and two of our three daughters were born here. This is where I live and expect to die someday.

My concern is that, unlike most nations, Americans can take such pride in being American that it can run to excess.

National pride can be a good thing. But the problem is, as the saying goes, "The good is the enemy of the best." Here in America we are almost to the point where I can hear us replacing Christ's statement about building His Church with, "I will build America and the gates of hell will not prevail against it."

As American Christians, I'm afraid we are guilty of "shrinking" the Church in our own minds. Only a few days ago I received an urgent request to pray from a group wanting to "reclaim America." While I appreciate their zeal I'm horrified that they are not wanting to apply equal zeal to "restoring the Church."

NO MORE NATIONAL VESSELS

During the period of time when the Old Testament was written, God had only one vessel in mind for accomplishing His purposes. That was the nation of Israel, and it was unique among the nations. Israel was to be among the other nations, but not one of them.

This is beautifully illustrated through Balaam's prophecy in Numbers 23. The Lord declares, "Behold, a people who dwells apart, and will not be reckoned among the nations" (Num. 23:9b). This special separateness was part of God's original plan, established long before in Abraham who was the founding father of the nation. God first separated Abraham from his friends and family. God was determined to have first place in his life and repeatedly tested Abraham's affections.

But at the birth of the Church, the special vessel became the Church. It is not that Israel has been forsaken or forgotten by God. Instead, the Church has become the vessel through which God's grace and will are now offered to the world. Israel, for its part, will be joined to the Church in due season.

Therefore, we who are in the Church today are to see that our first loyalty is not to this life, and our first citizenship is not in a country. Rather, we're to be loyal to Heaven and our first citizenship is to be in the Church. We are part of the vast family of God, "called out" from every kindred, tribe, and nation. This spiritual family is looked upon by God as His "holy nation." Family ties are greater than natural citizenship. I'm British, my wife is American, but our marriage and love for each other transcend nationality.

THE WHOLE BODY OF CHRIST

It's time we begin to recognize that God's purposes will only, and can only, be fulfilled through the Church. For the Church alone is the unique vessel that God has chosen to work through.

Watchman Nee expresses it this way in his book, *The Prayer Ministry of the Church*:

> We need to see that in all things that God does on earth today, He will first get the Church to stand with Him, and then He will do the work through her. God will not execute anything independently: whatever He does today, He does with the cooperation of the Church. She is that through which God manifests himself.[1]

I believe it's time for the Church to cast aside its inferiority complex and be the Church. Thank God for America and the faith of our founding fathers. Thank God for Columbus and his dreams. But we make the Church inferior when we submit it to national agendas, or when we mistake ourselves and only those like us to be "the Church." When all is said and done, the only instrument God intended to accomplish His purpose through, was and still is, the Church.

The Church is, and always will be, primary. We are His holy nation called to "proclaim the excellencies of Him who has called [us] out of darkness into His marvelous light" (1 Pet. 2:9b).

GETTING BACK TO BEING THE CHURCH

As we noted earlier, sometimes "the good" is the enemy of "the best." And what better strategy could the enemy use to divert our attention away from what God intended us to be than to enmesh us in "good" causes? The grave danger is that, when we become identified with causes, good though they might be, we may forget that we are first and foremost to be identified with Christ.

In America, the Christian community has poured multiplied millions into Christian politics with the hope that somehow we can make a difference. That is what I mean by becoming enmeshed in "the good." The best, however, can be achieved without spending a dime. It's as simple as humbling ourselves and praying.

Please don't think that I'm against believers being in politics. I'm not. I understand that God raises up individuals like Joseph, Esther, and Daniel and brings them into the Kingdom "for such a time as this." I am trying, however, to redirect our attention and energies back to the importance and power that God has invested in us, the Church.

The New Testament word for Church is the Greek word *ecclesia*, which means "a called-out company or assembly." In Greek secular society, this word signified those citizens within a city who were free and could vote. In other words, they alone held the power to make changes. They became the governing body of the city or province. What an incredible revelation we have here of God's purpose for His people!

Before God could begin His purpose through Abraham He first had to dislodge him from his family, friends, and country. That is because God intended him to form a new nation under His divine authority. This nation would be used to accomplish His purposes on earth. God called this nation to a place of preeminence—to be "the head and not the tail" (see Deut. 28:13). God's covenant promise to Abraham included the words "and your seed shall posses the gate of their enemies" (Gen. 22:17; 24:60). This nation was to bear testimony to His name throughout all the other nations. (See Isaiah 42:6-7; 49:6.)

A HIGH AND HOLY CALLING

God has called out the Church in order that we should continue in the high and holy calling of bearing testimony to the living Christ as His Spirit works to make Him known as the Lord of salvation throughout the whole earth.

It's time for the Church to arise and take her rightful place, which is following at His side, acting in obedience to his directives alone. The apostle Paul expresses it this way: "[He has] raised us up with Him, and seated us with Him in the heavenly places in Christ Jesus" (Eph. 2:6). As believers we need a fresh revelation of where we are spiritually positioned in Christ—that is, walking with the One in whom is all power and authority.

Tragically, this is not the vision of reality that is presented to most believers. At present the Church is far from being the instrument God intends it to be. Jesus made clear to His followers that they were to reflect His light, and be the light of this world. We are to be messengers of His saving power and the preserving salt of the earth.

Rather than exposing darkness, however, we have allowed the darkness of worldly thinking to invade the Church. We've taken our eyes off the One who is the Light of the world; instead of following Him in careful, humble obedience, we've adopted the "success formulas" valued by the world in order to feed our own pride.

As for being the preserving salt of the earth, we've also failed. We are not even preserving our marriages and families. The divorce rate among Christians, according to a recent survey, was higher among Christians in the "Bible Belt" than anywhere else in America. Salt is not only used to preserve, but to cause thirst. Here again, we have failed. Rather than the world wanting what the Church has, the Church is thirsting for what the world can offer.

HARSH LIGHT...HEALING LIGHT

When you cause someone to look at unhappy realities it's like forcing them to look at matters in a harsh light. But light that exposes hard truths is also the light that leads us on to our healing.

Today, we in the Body of Christ need to have our eyes turned away from the paths we've been following. We need to turn our heads from the world's images of success and lift the eyes of our spirits once again to fix them on the risen Lord. We need to follow Him, obeying the one and only Light of the world as He works by His Spirit to make the way of salvation known through us, His Body here on earth.

In the next chapter, we will begin to carefully consider what Jesus Christ has been saying to His Church. In particular, we'll consider what it means for us to follow the One who is the Light of the world...and to let His light shine in us.

ENDNOTE

1. Watchman Nee, *The Prayer Ministry of the Church* (New York: Christian Fellowship Publishers, Inc., 1975), p. 19.

CHAPTER 4

HIGH PRIEST OF THE LAMPS

I turned to see the voice that was speaking with me...and I saw seven golden lampstands; and in the middle...[stood] one like a son of man... (Revelation 1:12-13).

ONE OF THE MANY RESPONSIBILITIES of the high priest during the Old Testament tabernacle period was that of trimming the lamps. Twice a day, both morning and evening, he was instructed by Moses to enter the Holy Place and trim the seven lamps of the golden lampstand. As with any lamp that burns oil, the wicks would need to be trimmed periodically. This involved removing any deposits that would build up on the wick itself; the end result being that the lamp burned brightly, giving off the required light necessary. If these deposits were not removed, the light gradually weakened, and ultimately, would go out, plunging everything into darkness.

In the opening scene of Revelation, we see our great High Priest, the Lord Jesus Christ, the Head of the Church, walking among the seven golden lamps. We learn that the lamps are churches, and the Lord is filling them with oil, trimming the wicks, lest the light weaken and go out...lest the place where they are set be plunged into darkness. (See Revelation 1:12-20.)

What a brilliant picture of the Lord's work among us, and of the Church's role in the world. We are to be the light that burns brightly in this world of spiritual darkness. To be His light has always been God's purpose for His people. The prophet Isaiah declared, "The Lord will rise upon you and His glory will appear upon you. Nations will come to your light, and kings to the brightness of your rising" (Isa. 60:2b-3).

The Church is the only visible expression of Christ in the world. Just as the lampstand's source of power came from the oil, so likewise, the Church's only light comes from the life and power of the Spirit of God within her. Without the infilling of the "oil" of His presence we cannot burn with His Spirit. As with the lamps of old that required constant attention from the high priest, so too does the Church. Here in this opening scene we see Jesus working on the lamps, removing the deposits, which were causing His Church to lose her light and testimony.

Why was He doing this work?

Because, then as now, the brilliancy that Christ intended His Church to radiate was lacking that consistency He longed for and expected of her.

With this in mind, it becomes clear how vitally important this passage in Revelation is with regard to the Church today. Here we have only the second time that Jesus spoke concerning His Church. The first time was during His earthly ministry, when He declared, "I will build My Church; and the gates of hell shall not prevail against it" (Mt. 16:18b KJV). Then approximately 60 years later, Jesus, now ascended, speaks for the second time concerning His Church.

What we find is that all is not well.

And so Jesus comes to lovingly but firmly reprove and direct the Church—to trim away and remove those areas that are contrary to His will. Also, as we'll see, He commends them for those deeds that allow His light to shine in them, and so, meet His approval. We are about to see the Church examined in a way that no one else has a right to do.

THE NEED FOR EXAMINATION

The medical profession has recently released a report encouraging people over 40 years of age to have what is known as an "electron beam tomography scan" (EBT). This scan provides a three-dimensional image of the body. The whole idea is to "expose" yourself entirely in order to find out what potential problems you might be facing in the future. Already, many large corporations are encouraging their executive personnel to have these examinations. A recent television documentary trumpeted the benefits of such programs. It cited several individuals who had undergone this procedure and had been shown to have potential, life-threatening diseases. Because of early detection, these potential problems had been diverted and their lives saved.

Let's be honest, the thought of being examined by the Lord is frightening to most of us. We would rather He not show up unannounced to examine us or our church. We would prefer to get things set up nicely, all in order, and successful looking...then have Him drop by for a quick once-over and approval. But this attitude is the wrong one. It's the attitude of self-sufficiency. It's the attitude that says, "Come look at what I've done for You, Lord, in Your name. Tell me that I've done a good job." It's the attitude that shows we have not relied on the Holy Spirit, but on our own ways of doing things.

Instead, we need to adopt the attitude that says, "Lord, come examine me. Examine the way things are done in this church. Show us where things have gone off in a wrong direction because we've failed to live in close relation to You, hearing Your voice, following Your constant directives."

Only the Lord can apply the loving and firm course of correction. Too many are the leaders, and everyday believers, who when they've sensed a lack of vitality in their midst, run off to seek the advice of some "successful ministry expert" as to how to correct their problem; but with disaster as the result.

EVERYONE HAS THEIR OWN BIAS

The medical profession is very much divided when it comes to prescribing treatment for certain ailments or problems. Take a persistent headache for instance. Who should you contact? The family doctor may prescribe some painkillers. The chiropractor will recommend some type of adjustment. Meanwhile, the nutritionist will tell you that you need to change your diet, while the optician will suggest that your headaches are caused by eyestrain and encourage you to purchase glasses. The psychiatrist, on the other hand, may suggest you need therapy because you are obviously caught up in a great deal of inner conflict. Each solution, by itself, may be totally wrong, or it may be a needed part of the whole answer.

Nearly the same thing happens in the Church. Every branch has its own way of doing things and its own solutions.

Imagine what would happen if, for instance, we were to send a Pentecostal to help a church from the more traditional or liturgical branch of Christianity where the leader and congregation are feeling dry and in need of direction. The Pentecostal's diagnosis may be somewhat biased and could go something like this: "What this church needs is some life. The service is slow, lethargic, and lacking vision. You need to unplug the old pipe organ and get a praise band in here. The pastor needs to lose the robes and dress more casually. And the worship leader needs to learn some great worship choruses."

On the other hand, if we were to send Dr. Evangelical to the Pentecostals, I'm sure his diagnosis could also reflect some bias. "What this church needs is some order. It's too wild. It lacks reverence. It's more like a circus than a church."

Do you get the point? We go about seeking and offering our own little, partial solutions to the problem, while the greater need often remains unaddressed. It is this type of bias, wrong diagnoses, and weak solutions that have helped to create the present confusion within the Church.

When we are lacking spiritual vitality, who do we listen to? Whose opinion is correct?

THE EXAMINER WHOSE OPINION MATTERS

The apostle John begins by introducing us to the only Examiner whose opinion matters—the Lord Jesus Christ Himself. Volumes could be written on this first chapter of Revelation alone. It is not my desire to go into great detail, but rather to highlight what I consider some of the most important truths.

John's address to the seven churches comes from the eternal God who is, who was, and who is to come (see Rev. 1:4). This is not some "Johnny come lately" who is still wet behind the ears, spouting off his opinions as to what is wrong with the

Church. John goes on to mention the seven Spirits of God in the same verse. Here, once again, we have the concept of fullness and completeness. As the Examiner of our spiritual health, His examination is thorough.

John also mentions Jesus Christ, the faithful witness (see Rev. 1:5). A witness can either be a blessing or a curse depending on whose side he's on or how well he recalls the events that he's testifying about. Leaving out a vital part of information could change the whole outcome of the trial. Not so with this case. Our witness is not only faithful, He is the most reliable witness of all.

It is vital that we understand that the One examining us and passing judgment on our state of health speaks from both a heavenly and an earthly advantage: He is Jesus Christ, the firstborn from the dead. Paul refers to Him as "the Man Christ Jesus" (see 1 Tim. 2:5). He too has been subject to every temptation you and I have. He knows our frame; He's walked in our shoes.

John also refers to our Examiner as the one who loves us (see Rev. 1:5). What a difference that makes! If there is any bias at all in this examination, it is that of love. Truth without love can be devastating. Truth spoken in love can be liberating. His love does not in any way compromise the truth but rather motivates it. Our Examiner is not a foe, but a friend. I would far rather have my friend take the witness stand than my foe.

John gives us even greater detail about this one who has come to examine the churches. He is "one like a son of man, clothed in a robe reaching to the feet, and girded across His chest with a golden sash" (Rev. 1:13b). The robe is not only symbolic of His royal dignity as the Ruler of the kings of the earth, but also speaks of His judicial authority.

G. Campbell Morgan states, "This robing of the Son of Man reveals His judicial position among the churches, and that all the exercise of judicial right is based upon the faithfulness of the eternal love." That He is girdled, or bound, across His breast is, Morgan writes, a symbol of His faithfulness and affection.[1]

John next describes, "His head and His hair were white like white wool, like snow" (Rev. 1:14a). This typifies maturity, wisdom, and understanding. Not only that, but white represents purity—free from taint or mixture of any kind.

"His eyes were like a flame of fire" (Rev. 1:14b). Fire not only speaks of light—light being that which dispels darkness bringing clarity and revelation—but also a fire that refines. Malachi described the Lord as a refiner's fire (see Mal. 3:2). For fire, when applied to gold, causes the dross to rise to the surface in order for it to be removed. Apart from the fire, the gold and dross cling together, dulling and diminishing the value of the gold. The fire reveals the mixture and brings about the process of separation. "Eyes of fire" speaks of His all-searching, penetrating gaze that reveals and exposes every hidden sin or motivation. As the writer of Hebrews tells us, "All things are open and laid bare to the eyes of Him with whom we have to do" (Heb. 4:13b). Following His opening remarks in each of the seven letters that are to come He states, "I *know....*" Nothing, absolutely nothing, escapes His gaze.

CHRIST'S DOMINION AND JUDGMENT

It is interesting that John notes, "His feet were like burnished bronze" (Rev. 1:15a). Feet speak of dominion, walk, and stability. The fact that they were burnished reveals Christ's absolute purity both in His walk and dominion. As He walks among the churches, He has the right to put all things under His feet; His authority is final and His judgment is pure.

In verse 15 we also read, "His voice was like the sound of many waters." What a magnificent picture of the blending together of all the previous voices down through history! The writer to the Hebrews expresses it best when he says, "God, after He spoke long ago to the fathers in the prophets in many portions and in many ways, in these last days has spoken to us in His Son..." (Heb. 1:1-2a). This mighty voice like the sound of many waters ties together all the previous voices into one, just as any mighty river contains the water from various streams that flow into it. His voice does not contradict His previous words spoken by His servants and prophets of old but rather is the blending of them into one. His voice remains the same because His standards and values have never changed.

"Out of His mouth," we read, "came a sharp two-edged sword..." (Rev. 1:16). His words cut both ways. He condemns and condones, praises and prosecutes, denounces and defends. His word is final; there are no appeals or retrials.

"His face was like the sun shining in its strength" (Rev. 1:16b). The sun reaches its strength between its rising and its setting. Christ is viewed here at the zenith of His brightness. This is His constant state; He has no variableness or shadow of turning. The Light of His wisdom and judgment neither rises nor sets. "I am the Lord, I change not" (Mal. 3:6a KJV).

What a glorious and yet fearful picture! This Judge is the absolute final authority. There is no injustice with Him. He cannot be bribed. He shows no partiality. Nothing is hidden from Him as He discerns the thoughts and intentions of the heart. His verdict is not based on opinion polls or denominational politics. He cannot be deceived or misled. There are no plea bargains nor personal favors nor are there statutes of limitations that limit His justice and provide a safe harbor for the offender. Tears and begging won't change His mind. Friends and family can't intervene. Popularity and size won't sway His verdict. Rich and poor, black and white, male and female, educated and uneducated will all be treated the same. Seniority will have no pull.

There is but one thing that will lessen His severity. James reveals this one "secret" when he writes, "Judgment will be merciless to the one who has shown no mercy; mercy triumphs over judgment" (Jas. 2:13).

LOVING CORRECTION

We have met our Examiner.

As we conclude this look at the eternal Judge, the Lord Jesus Christ, we may be tempted to fear. We may want to hide in shame. There is no need. "Whatever was written in earlier times was written for our instruction..." (Rom. 15:4).

When the Lord examines us, as we are about to see, He does so to offer loving correction, and the promise of reward.

ENDNOTE

1. G. Campbell Morgan, *The Letters of Our Lord* (London: Pickering & Inglis, Ltd., n.d.), p. 14.

CHAPTER 5

THE EXAM BEGINS

IMAGINE YOU ARE ABOUT TO SIT FOR THE EXAMINATION of your life. The outcome is going to determine your entire future. You're not assured of being able to take it again should you fail. Some have passed with flying colors; others have failed completely. The standards have not been compromised in over two thousand years. The exam remains unchanged throughout every generation. And now your turn is coming.

Your hands become clammy; your heart races; your mind reels; perspiration breaks upon your forehead. Night after night you turn restlessly on your bed, your pillow damp from sweat. Nothing seems to relieve the anxiety or worry. The days begin to pass likes minutes as you head towards that dreaded moment when, suddenly, you're given an unbelievable gift. The Examiner sends you a copy of the exam. You can't believe your eyes. You think you're dreaming, but, no, it's true. You're actually holding in your hands the very test paper itself. What an incredible break. Best of all—it's legal!

MAJORING IN THE MINORS

Excitedly you begin poring over the paper convinced that you are just in need of brushing up on a few areas and well confident that your worries have been largely unfounded. As you read over the exam, however, your heart sinks.

You suddenly become aware of how little value you have placed on certain areas. The things you've majored on and considered important don't seem to appear anywhere, while the areas you have given little attention to are found throughout most of the exam. You realize that you have majored on the minors and neglected the things that are most important to the Examiner Himself.

You're grateful for one thing—you have a little time to "cram" (in Britain we say "swat") for the exam. But most of all, you're eternally grateful for the kindness of the Examiner who allowed you to see the paper ahead of time.

Now, every day you give yourself to studying the exam, determined that you are not going to waste a minute. Over and over you think to yourself, *I can't believe nobody told me these things.* You finally come to the conclusion that so many of your friends actually pointed you in the wrong direction, and that if you had listened to them, your name eventually would have been on the failure list.

THERE IN BLACK AND WHITE

What you have just read is not simply conjecture on my part but is, in fact, true when it comes to our relationship with the Lord. We will be examined to see if we have been following Him, in obedience to His ways; or if we have been building in His name...but in our own way. These seven letters to the churches of Asia Minor have been passed down to us through the kindness and generosity of the Examiner Himself. They were written for our instruction. If you listen carefully you can hear His firm but loving voice correcting and redirecting us.

Yes, God's current message to the Church is all here in black and white. This is the more sure Word of prophecy. It is the Word that will be the standard against which we are examined. Jesus made this absolutely clear when He said, "He who rejects Me and does not receive My sayings, has one who judges him; the word I spoke is what will judge him at the last day" (Jn. 12:48).

If that isn't enough to convince you, then look again at the first few verses of Revelation where John writes, "Blessed is he who reads and those who hear the words of the prophecy and heed [keep] the things which are written in it; for the time is near" (Rev. 1:3).

LIVING IN LIGHT OF ETERNITY

What "time" is John talking about? I believe he is talking about the time in each of our lives when we enter eternity. The exam will be over, and there we will have to face the Examiner.

If this is unsettling to you, it need not be. Personally I am grateful for the reminders of eternity in my life.

About two years ago, my wife and I purchased my parents' home in Texas. The home is just an average ranch-style home, but I now have the joy of occupying my father's study. It was here he prayed and wrote. Ministers gathered weekly for prayer. People came from across the nation and from around the world to talk with my father about revival and prayer. The office is still lined with thousands of books and several plaques with just the word "eternity" on them. *Eternity* was my father's favorite word. He lived his life in the light of eternity. Somehow he had risen above the realm of the temporal and entered the realm of the eternal.

Eternity sheds new understanding on our values. The songwriter expressed it well when he wrote,

> Perishing things of clay,
> Born but for one brief day,
> Take from my heart away—
> Jesus is mine!

Jesus said it best when He taught, "Lay not up for yourself treasures upon earth, where moth and rust [destroy], and where thieves break through and steal: But lay up for yourselves treasures in heaven…" (Mt. 6:19-20a KJV).

The thought of facing Christ, our Examiner, in eternity need not be dismaying—not if you have heeded His words. Those leading the Church, and everyone else doing other work of the Church, are simply asked to listen and obey. It is that simple.

TAKING STOCK NOW

I want to ask at this point: Are you living your life in light of eternity? If you are a spiritual leader, or a hardworking member of a church, are you building the Church in light of Christ's standards?

Consider the old song, "This world is not my home, I'm just a-passing through." Does this express the way you think and live? Does it describe the attitude you take in building the Church of our Lord Christ? Or have you become conformed to this world, measuring your "success" by the world's temporal values?

As we consider these seven letters, we're about to see that the Examiner of our works grades on a scale that is much different from the one we use here on earth. But that shouldn't really surprise us; after all, Jesus has said all along, "The last shall be first, and the first last" (Mt. 20:16); "Blessed are [you], when men shall revile you, and persecute you, and shall say all manner of evil against you..." (Mt. 5:11 KJV); "Love your enemies and pray for those who persecute you..." (Mt. 5:44b).

Heaven most certainly has a different perspective.

Are you willing now to reexamine your own life and work in the light of Christ's standards for His Church?

CHAPTER 6

THE SEVEN ANGELS

WE HAVE BUILT UP A LOT OF ANTICIPATION to this point, preparing to hear what the Spirit is saying to the churches. And yet, before we look at these seven messages, we need to pause one last time and consider to whom the Lord is addressing these urgent letters containing the standards by which we will be examined.

John tells us the Lord is speaking to the seven "stars" or "angels" of the churches (see Rev. 1:20).

WHO ARE THE STARS...OR ANGELS...OF THE CHURCHES?

By "stars" I'm afraid we're tempted to think of the Hollywood-type stars—gifted, favored, "beautiful" people whom everyone admires and to whom everyone defers. That is not what's meant here, as we'll see in a moment.

The angels John refers to are not what we normally think of either. These angels don't have wings or dwell in Heaven. These are very much earthly "angels"—they signify spiritual leaders. How do we know that? Very simply, by looking at the letters addressed to them. Of the seven personalities addressed, four have need of repentance and all are exhorted to overcome. While we may be able to excuse some from the need of repentance, all are told to overcome. This cannot be applied to celestial angels.

In addition, why are these spiritual leaders referred to as "stars"?

Primarily, because God created stars to give light to the earth during the dark times. It is the spiritual leader's responsibility to shed light amid the surrounding darkness of the world. Daniel expresses it well: "Those who have insight will shine brightly like the brightness of the expanse of heaven, and those who lead the many to righteousness, like the stars forever and ever" (Dan. 12:3).

Stars are also used to provide guidance. Sailors have used stars to chart their course for centuries. Jude takes up this image and uses it in the negative sense when he speaks concerning those who have crept into the Church to mislead and deceive the flock. He refers to them as "wandering stars" (see Jude 13).

The seven stars John saw were held in the right hand of the risen Christ. This fact is mentioned twice. What significance can we learn from this? I have pondered many times on this passage and especially this one phrase—"the seven stars...in My right hand" (Rev. 1:20a). And I am convinced there are vital truths that those who are in positions of spiritual leadership, especially, need to grasp...though there are truths here for all of us.

SPIRITUAL LEADERS HAVE A PLACE OF SECURITY

Leaders need to understand that if they have truly been appointed by God, they don't need to feel threatened by anyone. My friend Mike Bickle once taught on the life of David, and zeroed in on the verse that says, "And David realized that the Lord had established him as king..." (2 Sam. 5:12). Mike reflected this unalterable truth: When God places you in leadership, nothing and no one can alter that fact. The only one who can change it is you—through sin and disobedience. And yet, so many leaders struggle with insecurity. They're hesitant to allow others to exercise their callings and gifts for fear they'll lose their position.

Every believer needs to know that we have a place of security in Christ, and a place in building His Church. And every leader needs to see that if they are truly called by God, they are held and therefore secure in the hands of the Lord.

SPIRITUAL LEADERS HAVE A PLACE OF INTIMACY

You cannot imagine this picture—the Lord Himself, holding the seven stars in His strong right hand—and miss the beauty of it. Christ, the ever-living Lord, holds you. Nothing speaks of intimacy like that. I think of the slogan that Allstate Insurance has used for years: "You're in good hands with Allstate." There is something so intimate here, as Christ places His hand around us and draws us to Himself.

Every leader needs to see himself in this place of intimacy. The gospels tell us that "[Jesus] appointed twelve, so that they would be with Him and that He could send them out to preach" (Mk. 3:14). Winkie Pratney says you have no authority to go out to preach unless you have spent intimate time with Him.

LEADERS HAVE A PLACE OF AUTHORITY

God's right hand invariably speaks of His power or authority. We have all been raised together and seated with Him on the right hand of God in heavenly places. But here we are held in His right hand. The right hand signifies authority.

As Rachel gave birth and died in the process, she named the child Ben-oni, "son of my sorrows." But Jacob gave him the special honor of calling him Benjamin, "son of my right hand" (see Gen. 35:18). Think of the honor Christ has given us as spiritual leaders to be held in His right hand, representative of His authority.

LEADERS HAVE A PLACE OF CLARITY

How different things appear when viewed from Heaven's perspective. Climb any mountain or, better yet, fly over the earth by plane, and you soon grasp how differently things appear from your higher vantage point.

I'm convinced that God wants to open our understanding as spiritual leaders to see things from His perspective. Isn't this the leader's main responsibility—to teach people the heavenly viewpoint? And yet we cannot proclaim it unless we have experienced it firsthand.

LEADERS HAVE A PLACE OF UNITY

In John's vision, the seven stars are all held by the same hand. John sees things here from his heavenly perspective. There are seven churches, each located in a different city, and yet from God's point of view they are all one.

Pastor, that leader down the road or across town is held in the same hand as you are. John doesn't describe a fight happening among the stars, but shows us the unity that God intends. Leaders desperately need to recognize that they are a part of the greater Body of Christ and that God's great longing, as revealed through the prayer of Jesus, is "that they may be one..." (Jn. 17:22b).

LEADERS ARE CALLED TO A PLACE OF PURITY

To see ourselves as God sees us should cause us to fear. We are riddled with impure thoughts and motives; yet how can a person even consider sinning while dwelling in such a close relationship with the Lord? Joseph's awareness of God's presence caused him to flee from the daily temptations of Potiphar's wife. When Moses drew close to the burning bush God spoke to him, "Remove your sandals from your feet, for the place on which you are standing is holy ground" (Ex. 3:5b).

As spiritual leaders, we are standing in the very presence of God and held within His own right hand. Yet only as our eyes are opened to this fact will we seek to walk in holiness before Him. Sadly, according to some statistics from Focus on the Family, some 18,000 ministers a year step down from ministry due to immorality or spiritual burnout.

LEADERS ARE CALLED TO A PLACE OF ASCENDANCY

Every leader needs to recognize the incredible privilege of being called into leadership. This is a high calling unsurpassed by any other. While Christ is portrayed as the Ruler of the kings of the earth, we have no similar picture in God's Word of Him holding kings in His right hand. No, this is a special and unique position reserved only for those leaders in His beloved Church.

We could no doubt expand further upon each of these insights. It is enough, I hope, to realize that we as spiritual leaders need to see ourselves as God sees us. What great peace and comfort to know we are held by Him. What strength comes from knowing His authority is the ground on which we stand.

Also, what a great challenge to know that we are called to shine with His light into a dark world. Only as we continue to behold Him, keeping our spiritual eyes turned to Him, following Him, can we continue to reflect His light, and refuse to go dim and burn out because we have left Him behind and gone our own way.

And now, let's turn to the letters Christ has written to the spiritual leaders of His Church.

CHAPTER 7

EPHESUS—THE "BIG SUCCESSFUL CHURCH"

Now we come to the all-important instructions given to the seven churches.

For those familiar with these chapters in Revelation, you know that the Lord's message to each church follows the same general course in each letter and uses the following outline:

His introduction.

His commendation.

His condemnation.

His exhortation.

I don't intend to follow the above outline rigidly while listening to what Christ says to His churches. Rather, I'll highlight certain areas for our consideration. I'll also add, it's not my purpose to go into the historical significance of each church and the city of its location. There are scores of books available detailing the cities themselves and the uniqueness of their settings and history, as well as expounding every phrase and word of the passage itself. My purpose is to examine each letter in order to grasp what Jesus Himself considered important and unimportant.

Let's begin with the first letter to the church at Ephesus.

THE CHURCH THAT LOOKED LIKE A DREAM

Ephesus was the type of church every pastor dreams of leading. There were no slackers here. Everyone was involved. You didn't find five percent of the people doing ninety-five percent of the work, because everyone was laboring together.

And speaking of work, they didn't just show up and somewhat begrudgingly do what was required of them. Not by a long stretch. This was a committed body of believers who worked long and hard, giving everything they had. Paul's influence had obviously worn off on them. He was no slouch when it came to work, many times ministering while still holding down a secular job. Here we see it in Paul's spiritual descendants. Jesus says, "I know your deeds and your toil" (Rev. 2:2a). The word *toil* according to G. Campbell Morgan means "effort that produces work even at the cost of pain."[1] Like spiritual Marines advancing forward to secure a beachhead, these believers worked on, regardless of the cost.

Jesus goes on to commend them for their patience. Most of us can give a little extra if we have to, but sustaining it over the long run is what separates the men from the boys. These believers knew how to run a marathon, not just some quick dash. There isn't a pastor anywhere that wouldn't welcome a few dozen members like this. Imagine what the Church would be like if every member had this type of zeal and tenacity?

In today's church world, this kind of dedication would draw ministers from around the world. "How to" seminars would be packed with eager listeners wanting to know how to duplicate this phenomenon in their congregations. This is the ultimate "church with a purpose," bursting at the seams, construction going on everywhere. This is the *happening place* to be.

Ephesus not only excelled in its work ethic, but also in its spiritual integrity. They prided themselves in their standard of holiness. Sin was dealt with immediately; they had no patience for it. Please keep in mind this is part of their commendation. It behooves us to know that we learn God's values by what He condones and what He condemns.

Yet how many churches today are lax when dealing with known sin? A pastor recently said to me how shocked he was to learn that there are a large percentage of active homosexuals involved in various church activities. Ephesus had high standards in this regard and received high marks also. Jesus is not coming back for a Church with the morals of Hollywood, but a holy Church. "Let everyone who names the name of Christ depart from iniquity" (2 Tim. 2:19b NKJV).

Thirdly, they are commended for conducting a test for those calling themselves apostles, but I will deal with this separately in another chapter. Much more could be said with regards to the virtues of this congregation. So far it excels in so many areas of service. I, for one, would be thrilled to lead a flock like this—or would I?

We now come to the pivotal point in this letter—the word "but."

You know immediately that when someone hands you a string of accolades followed by a "but," you're about to hear what is really on that person's mind. I rather think this is the case here.

LEAVING YOUR FIRST LOVE

"But I have this against you," says the Lord, "that you have left your first love" (Rev. 2:4).

One of the difficulties with any written message, as opposed to that spoken, is that we miss the feeling behind the words. If only we could capture the pathos. Here we have the Bridegroom speaking to the bride. He remembers a time when their relationship was alive with fervor, feeling, and passion. Hours together seemed like minutes. Everything else paled in importance to being together. This is the voice of the lonely Lover who recalls the past and wonders what went wrong.

In Ephesus, something has changed from the early days when everything about their faith was fresh and new. Their lives had been made new by the washing of regeneration. Their worship was spontaneous, filled with emotion and expressions of thanksgiving. There was a hunger for God's Word. Like newborn babes they were constantly craving the Word, drinking it in with an insatiable appetite. Everything they did was done to please their Lover and Master. No task was too trivial. They were eager to convey how deeply they felt for their Beloved. Their passion was pure, their priorities right. Jesus Christ was central and supreme in every thought and action. Truly He had come to have first place in everything.

Now their passion has been replaced with other priorities. There is work to be done—a world to win. Doctrinal purity has replaced devotional passion. The letter of the word is now far more important than the Spirit of the Word. Worship has given place to work. Their love has begun to go cold as the chill of ritualism has begun. Hearts that once thrilled at the mention of Christ's name have turned to pride, as they boast of their ability to hunt down heretics and test apostles.

The best way to describe this church is to liken it to an expensive engagement ring crafted by a leading jeweler. The workmanship is exquisite. Every stone is cut perfectly and set so as to enhance the overall appearance. And yet something is missing—there is no central stone, just empty prongs.

The Ephesian church had many fine and admirable qualities, but the central stone of love had been lost. Paul expresses it so well when writing to the Corinthians, saying, "If I speak with the tongues of men and of angels, but do not have love, I have become a noisy gong or a clanging cymbal" (1 Cor. 13: 1). We could add: If I labor to extend God's Kingdom, even working long hours and with painful toil, and though I rid the church of evil men and test those who call themselves apostles, and yet have lost my first love, it profits me nothing.

Luke gives us a glimpse of this same problem in microcosm, when he shows us the Church represented by "two or three gathered together." In Luke 10:38-42, we read that Jesus is visiting the house of Mary and Martha. Mary's only interest is Jesus. She is content just to sit at His feet and listen. Martha in the meantime is busy, very busy, no doubt working at something that she hoped would find approval sometime later. Perhaps it was a meal she was fussing over or some last-minute decorations that in her mind were essential. Her frustration and impatience is revealed when she says to Jesus, "Lord, do You not care that my sister has left me to do all the serving alone?" Jesus responds so lovingly, "Martha, Martha, you are worried and bothered about so many things; but only one thing is necessary...Mary has chosen the good part...."

The Church desperately needs to understand the value that Jesus places upon devoting ourselves to Him—making Him our "first love." In the Western Church especially, we have become "distracted with all our preparations." Like Martha, we fail to understand the importance of sitting at His feet. This, I believe, was Paul's intention when he wrote to the Colossians, exhorting them to keep their priorities right: "He is also head of the body, the church; and He is the beginning, the firstborn from the dead, so that He Himself will come to have first place in everything" (Col. 1:18).

John MacArthur, Jr., in his wonderful book *The Ultimate Priority*, tells the following story:

> A number of years ago I read a newspaper account of a christening party in a wealthy Boston suburb. The parents had opened their palatial home to friends and relatives who had come to celebrate the wonderful event. As the party was moving along and the people were having a wonderful time, eating and drinking and celebrating and enjoying one another, somebody said, "By the way, where is the baby?"
>
> The heart of that mother jumped and she instantly left the room, rushing into the master bedroom where she had left the baby asleep in the middle of the massive bed. The baby was dead, smothered by the many coats of the guests.[2]

How easily we become caught up in the work of the ministry and yet miss ministering to the Master Himself. Morgan said, "No amount of activity in the King's service will make up for the neglect of the King."[3]

OUR ONE GOAL

For the past number of years I have carried in my Bible a small piece of paper that I tore from a calendar. On every page there was a saying for that day. What I read left a huge impression in my spirit. I pray that I will never forget the underlying thought I read. Here is what it said:

I believe with all my heart that it is impossible to be both goal-oriented and God-oriented at the same time. One orientation will always take precedence over the other. When our desire to achieve takes the lead, several things happen in our relationship with God. He becomes a means to an end rather than the end. We tend to use God rather than worship him. We find ourselves seeking *information about* Him rather than *transformation by* him.[4]

There is a deception that comes with any emphasis on service; the lie is that service to God can be measured both by numbers and results. We subtly become like the Pharisee who prided himself on being spiritual because he fasted and paid tithes. His works, in his own mind, were evidence of his spirituality.

The intensity of "first love," however, cannot be measured by numbers or programs. Nor can it be valued by budgets or buildings. We deceive ourselves if we look at a marriage as being great based solely on the size of the house, the spouse's income, or the size of the family. None of these visible assets reveal the love the couple shares together.

First love transcends all other affections. Jesus said, "He who loves father or mother more than Me is not worthy of Me; and he who loves son or daughter more than Me is not worthy of Me. And he who does not take his cross [death to love of self] and follow after Me is not worthy of Me" (Mt. 10:37-38).

First love also transcends the love of things. John writes, "Do not love the world nor the things in the world. If anyone loves the world, the love of the Father is not in him" (1 Jn. 2:15). James takes it a step farther, "You adulteresses, do you not know that friendship with the world is hostility toward God? Therefore, whoever wishes to be a friend of the world makes himself an enemy of God" (Jas. 4:4). Paul adds this word of warning to his son, Timothy, concerning the last days, "For men will be lovers of self, lovers of money...lovers of pleasure rather than lovers of God" (2 Tim. 3:2-4).

First love is measured by priority, intensity, quality, and purity. Paul, speaking to the Corinthians, tells them, "For I am jealous for you with a godly jealousy; for I betrothed you to one husband, so that to Christ I might present you as a pure virgin" (2 Cor. 11:2). G. Campbell Morgan writes, "First love is the abandonment of all for a love that has abandoned all." He continues, "All zeal for the Master that is not the outcome of love is worthless."[5]

Allow me to take this one step further. When we speak about love, we can readily fall into a subtle trap of deception that lulls us into a false security and thereby weakens our love. Let me explain what I mean.

We all know of the unconditional love God has toward us. Regardless of what we do, God still loves us. But we need to realize that there is a vast difference between His love for us and His pleasure in us. This is best illustrated in Malachi chapter 1. God makes clear through His prophet that He loves His people: " 'I have loved you,' says the Lord" (Mal. 1:2a). Yet a few verses later He states, "I am not pleased with you..." (Mal. 1:10b). First love is that quality of love that seeks to please God in everything we do.

"MARRIAGE COUNSELING" FOR THE CHURCH

While I would not consider myself much of a marriage counselor, I have many times over the course of my ministry referred couples to what I consider to be some of the best marriage advice I have ever read. Strange as it may seem, this advice is given by the apostle Paul, in the passage in which he encourages singles to remain single. (See First Corinthians 7.) He says, "One who is married is concerned about the things of the world, how he may please his wife" (1 Cor. 7:33). Then, referring to the woman, he writes the same, "...how she may please her husband" (1 Cor. 7:34). So often, marriage is entered into from a selfish standpoint, looking for a partner to meet your needs, rather than living to please your partner.

This, I believe, is what the Lord desires for His "marriage"—a people whose one goal is to bring pleasure to the heart of God. We see this expressed in Jesus' life when He says, "I always do the things that are pleasing to [the Father]" (Jn. 8:29b). The Father states of His Son, "You are My beloved Son, in You I am well-pleased" (Lk. 3:22b). Paul caught this glorious revelation when, in writing to the Colossians, he states, "So that you will walk in a manner worthy of the Lord, to please Him in all respects..." (Col. 1:10).

The Ephesian church had fallen from this type of relationship and was told to repent. Her first love had been eclipsed by doctrine, discipline, and duty.... and no longer by devotion. One has to constantly guard their relationship lest it becomes one of law rather than love. The Ephesians were legally blameless and to all outward appearances perfect, but those all-seeing eyes of the Master longed again for the days when their hearts were aflame with passion for His glorious presence. As Paul writes to the Thessalonians, "We give thanks to God always for you...bearing in mind your work of *faith* and labor of *love* and steadfastness of *hope*" (1 Thess. 1:2-3a). This reveals the difference between the Thessalonians and the Ephesians. The

Ephesians were said to have these same virtues but without the *faith, love,* and *hope.*

When our work for God is lacking in *faith,* our labor is performed without *love,* and our perseverance is without *hope,* then we too have left our first love. And as Morgan states it so well, "Without first love we may retain ceaseless activity, immaculate purity, severest orthodoxy, but there will be no love shining in a dark place."[6]

ENDNOTES

1. G. Campbell Morgan, *The Letters of Our Lord* (London: Pickering & Inglis, Ltd., n.d.), p. 22.

2. John MacArthur, Jr., *The Ultimate Priority* (Chicago: Moody Press, 1983), p. 21.

3. Morgan, p. 27.

4. Charles Stanley, *A Touch of His Freedom* (Grand Rapids, MI: Zondervan Publishing, 1991), n.p.

5. Morgan, pp. 25, 27.

6. *Ibid.,* p. 30.

CHAPTER 8

WILL THE REAL APOSTLES
PLEASE STAND UP?

PATRICK AND BARBARA SELDOM MISSED a Sunday service. You could always tell they were there because their family—including all ten children—made quite an entrance. For almost five years, as their pastor, I don't ever recall hearing Patrick having to defend the fact that he was indeed father to these children. Every one of them, in his or her own face, bore testimony to it. Each one reflected the image of their father.

In the Spirit's letter to the church in Ephesus an important point is made about the testing of "those who call themselves apostles" (see Rev. 2:2). The question that occupied them constantly, it appears, and took so much of their energy, was: Who is a real apostle of Jesus Christ, and who is an impostor? I believe this is such an important topic in itself because it is relevant to the Church today and requires some very careful attention.

The term "apostle," in reference to a current ministry, is actually only being used in the charismatic and Pentecostal branches of the Church. If you're reading this book and you're not of that persuasion you might be tempted to skip over this chapter...but I encourage you not to. Experience tells me that in every branch of the Church, including the Evangelical and the Liturgical, there are people who are looked up to as over-leaders—that is, leaders to establish, train, and encourage other leaders. Allow me to succinctly define the fivefold ministry given to the Church by Christ, as listed in Ephesians 4:11: The apostle *governs*; the prophet *guides*; the evangelist *gathers*; the pastor *guards*; and the teacher *grounds*.

It is important for us all, therefore, to understand the role of the apostle.

APOSTLES TODAY

Apostolic ministry is currently a major topic, especially, as I've noted, in certain parts of the Body of Christ. Web sites devoted to the "apostolic" number in the thousands. Only yesterday, I typed into my computer the words "apostolic ministry," and it listed some 46,000 references.

Yet there seems to be so much insecurity among today's apostolic ministries. Why, when it comes to "apostolic ministry," does everyone suddenly become so defensive? Why are so many insistent upon being recognized and honored? If you are an apostle, you will be known by your works—for "you will know them by their fruits" (Mt. 7:16a).

OUR ONE TRUE STANDARD

The Ephesians had the same problem we are about to have or already have. How do you tell a real apostle from a false one? Because the Ephesians were commended for testing those who called themselves *apostle,* we need to recognize that this should also be true of the Church today. Where then do we begin?

First of all, Scripture makes it clear that the fivefold ministry is God's gift to the Church. It was in his letter to the Ephesians that Paul clearly taught that "[the Lord] gave some as apostles...for the equipping of the saints for the work of service, to the building up of the body of Christ" (Eph. 4:11-12). Referring to his own apostleship, he states in his letter to the Galatians, "Paul, an apostle (not from men nor through the agency of man, but through Jesus Christ and God the Father...)" (Gal. 1:1). Paul made it clear that he was not a self-appointed apostle nor was he appointed by man. Paul was appointed by God Himself.

Yet, today, we have self-appointed apostles, as well as ministries, who travel around and appoint others as apostles.

On a recent trip to Spain, I talked with the pastor of a growing church where they were experiencing a real touch of God in their midst. During the course of our conversation, he mentioned some well-known ministries that had ministered in Spain over the past year. One ministry team in particular had caused him some concern. This team, a man and woman, were prophesying over certain individuals and calling them forth into their apostolic roles. This type of activity is not only dangerous, but unbiblical. If God's Word requires "elders" to be subject to certain standards prior to being set into office, what right do we have to prophesy over people who are totally unknown and confer upon them the office of an apostle? Where in God's Word do we find a precedent for such behavior?

The Ephesian church was commended for testing those claiming to be apostles. As we don't have a record of what this test consisted of, we need to establish some basis upon which to make our judgment. There is only one standard by which we judge truth—the Word of God, the Truth itself. The best way to spot a fake is to compare it with the real item. The only way to expose a false apostle is to compare him to the true Apostle, Jesus Christ Himself.

The writer to the Hebrews refers to Jesus as "the Apostle and High Priest..." (Heb. 3:1b). Following are His qualifications.

First: He was sent by God.

- "As the Father has sent Me, I also send you" (Jn. 20:21b).

- "I have come...not to do My own will, but the will of Him who sent Me" (Jn. 6:38).

- "The Spirit of the Lord is upon Me, because He anointed Me to preach..." (Lk. 4:18a).

Jesus was not self-appointed or self-anointed. Beware of those who appoint themselves apostles!

Second: He came to serve.

- "If I then, the Lord and the Teacher, washed your feet, you also ought to wash one another's feet" (Jn. 13:14).

- Who, although He existed in the form of God, did not regard equality with God a thing to be grasped, but emptied Himself, taking the form of a bond servant... (Phil. 2:6-7a).

- "Whoever wishes to be first among you shall be [servant] of all" (Mk. 10:44).

Beware of the "apostle" who doesn't possess a servant's heart!

Third: He walked in humility.

- "Take My yoke upon you and learn from Me, for I am gentle and humble in heart" (Mt. 11:29a).

- Behold your king is coming to you; He is just...humble, and mounted on a donkey (Zech. 9:9b).

- "And you will never again be haughty on My holy mountain. But I will leave among you a humble and lowly people" (Zeph. 3:11b-12a).

- "If anyone wants to be first, he shall be last of all and servant of all" (Mk. 9:35b).

- God has appointed in the church, first apostles... (1 Cor. 12:28).

- For, I think, God has exhibited us apostles last of all....we are weak but you are strong; you are distinguished, but we are without honor (1 Cor. 4:9-10).

- From these verses (1 Cor. 4:9-10; 12:28) we understand that apostles are first in *position* and last in *privilege*.

- Diotrephes...loves to be first... (3 Jn. 9b).

Beware of the man who always wants to be first; whose title produces pride, not humility!

Fourth: He has a shepherd's heart.

- "He calls His own sheep by name and leads them out" (Jn. 10:3b).

- "I am the good shepherd; the good shepherd lays down His life for the sheep" (Jn. 10:11).

- Seeing the people, He felt compassion for them, because they were distressed and dispirited like sheep without a shepherd (Mt. 9:36).

Beware of the man who doesn't know your name and is not willing to lay down his life for you!

Fifth: He loved every type of person.

• ...a friend of tax collectors and sinners (Lk. 7:34).

• Jesus said, "Let the children alone, and do not hinder them from coming to Me" (Mt. 19:14a).

• "The poor have the gospel preached to them" (Lk. 7:22b).

Beware of the person who surrounds himself with only the rich and famous but has little time for the common man.

Sixth: He gave of His personal substance to help others.

• Though He was rich, yet for your sake He became poor... (2 Co. 8:9b).

• "Upon finding one pearl of great value, he went and sold all that he had and bought it" (Mt. 13:46).

• "Take care of him; and whatever more you spend, when I return I will repay you" (Lk. 10:35b).

Beware of the man whose only interest is your money.

Seventh: He was a man of prayer.

• It happened that while Jesus was praying in a certain place... (Lk. 11:1).

• "Sit here while I go over there and pray" (Mt. 26:36b).

• In the early morning...Jesus got up, left the house, and went away to a secluded place, and was praying there (Mk. 1:35).

Beware of the one who is seldom seen praying!

Eighth: He wasn't impressed with titles.

- "They love the place of honor...and respectful greet-ings...and being called Rabbi by men. But do not be called Rabbi...Whoever exalts himself shall be hum-bled..." (Mt. 23:6-12).

- "I do not receive glory from men" (Jn. 5:41).

Beware of the person who insists on being recognized as an apostle!

There are many other outstanding attributes that we could consider regarding the Chief Apostle, the Lord Jesus Christ. The greater the apostle, the greater his Christlikeness is evident. Paul was able to say, "Be imitators of me, just as I also am of Christ" (1 Cor. 11:1). Few would doubt that, aside from the Lord, Paul is considered one of the greatest apostles of all time. His life, therefore, needs careful consideration, if we are to understand the true nature of an apostle.

Beware of the man you can't imitate!

PAUL—AN EXEMPLARY APOSTLE

Paul was far more concerned about the spiritual care of the flock than he was in wielding his apostolic authority. Apos-tolic authority without the heart of a shepherd can lend itself to dangerous abuse of power. The sheep are first taught to sub-mit to authority. Once that foundation is laid in their thinking, the one having authority is free to "crack the whip" in any way he desires. After all, to question his leadership is to be in re-bellion. This type of arrangement is neither good for the leader or those allotted to his care. This leaves the sheep with no voice and the leader with no accountability.

There is a common tendency today for a so-called "chief apostle" to only relate to his spiritual appointee, the local pastor (a budding apostle himself). These men of God are in constant contact with each other, forever gathering in their spiritual huddles to plan the next great play. Seldom, if ever, do the members of the congregation have opportunity to relate to them. This, in turn, leads again to spiritual abuse as all the pastor has to do is turn in a good report to his apostolic oversight, who then assumes everything is going okay. Every so-called apostolic leader should spend time in open discussion hearing from the sheep themselves. I know of leaders who spend more time outside their pulpits than they do behind them. Some even go so far as to tell their congregations that they are not pastors, but rather called to "put the church in order." This is akin to a father calling together his children and telling them he's not their father, but at the same time goes around telling others how to raise their kids.

Every apostle must have a shepherd's heart. Paul demonstrated this continually. When addressing the elders of the church in Ephesus, he warned them, "I know that after my departure savage wolves will come in among you, not sparing the flock; and from among your own selves men will arise, speaking perverse things, to draw away the disciples after them" (Acts 20:29-30). Paul's heart was first and foremost concerned about the spiritual well-being of his flock.

We can also learn much about the character and compassion of Paul in the first two chapters of his first letter to the Thessalonians. Here we find the *real deal*. Those claiming apostolic gifting would do well to compare themselves to him.

- He gave thanks for every one of them.

- He prayed for them all night and day.

- They were foremost on his mind, out of his love and concern.

- His messages were not just in word only, but in power resulting in conviction.

- His life was an example for them to imitate.

- He envisioned them to impact their world around them.

- He endured personal suffering and mistreatment.

- He refused to use error or devious means to exhort them.

- He sought only God's approval, not man's.

- He refused to allow greed to play any role in his ministry.

- He wasn't driven by popularity.

- He restrained his apostolic authority.

- He, instead, used a gentle approach, acting like a mother with a newborn.

- He was motivated by deep love and affection, not by power.

- He not only imparted the gospel, but laid down his own life.

- He worked day and night so as not to place a financial burden upon them.

- He conducted himself with integrity, walking blamelessly among them.

- He reasoned with them as a father would with his own children.

- He longed for them to mature and walk worthy of the Lord.

- He derived his joy from their spiritual growth and well-being.

Here we see a man with a single focus—the well-being of his flock. He was not driven by greed or popularity. We don't find him flying his own plane and living high on the hog. No. Here was this renowned apostle working a secular job so as not to burden the flock. He was more concerned about their spiritual growth than the size of his bank account.

Today, many so-called apostles refuse to minister without first having some guaranteed amount. I, personally, would not allow this type of behavior in any church I pastor.

Following are some warning signs that signal the presence of a false apostle:

1. They pride themselves on being called apostles.

2. They boast about how many churches, ministries, or missions they have under their direction.

3. They talk more about *their* agenda than extending the Kingdom of God.

4. They seek to draw people to themselves instead of to God.

5. They place undue emphasis on money.

6. They use teachings about "covering" as a means of control.

7. They relate only to other leaders who hold the same views as theirs.

8. They have little pastoral gifting.

9. They give the impression that they alone know the voice of God in a given situation.

10. They are quick to reject you if your opinions differ from theirs.

11. They have no accountability themselves.

13. They live lifestyles well above the majority of their flock.

In order to justify their lavish lifestyles, many ministries quote Paul's first letter to Timothy. When addressing the matter of elders/leaders, Paul says they are worthy of "double honor" (see 1 Tim. 5:17). Many interpret this to mean double the salary of the average person. I believe the double honor simple refers to having a salary. The first honor is that of the office itself.

CONCLUSION

What we have now are some solid standards by which we can recognize the leader who has a true apostolic role and the one who does not. I believe the Spirit is still saying to the Church that it is a good thing to have solid standards to follow. Not all who try to step into positions as leaders of other leaders are ready or deserving of such responsibility.

And now that we have considered this important matter, let's return to Revelation and consider other significant issues about which the Spirit of Christ is speaking to the churches.

CHAPTER 9

SMYRNA—THE RICH-IN-SPIRIT CHURCH

PAUL MARSHALL, IN HIS BOOK *Their Blood Cries Out,* tells us:

> There are some 200 million Christians worldwide undergoing some form of persecution. The U.S. State Department cites over sixty countries where Christians face the realities of massacre, rape, torture, mutilation, family division, harassment, imprisonment and slavery, as well as discrimination in education and employment and even death.[1]

Here in the Western Church, persecution is having to sit in a church with air conditioning problems and having to endure an hour with temperatures in the high 70s. For others, it's speaking up in public debate, letting our Christian views be known, only to be ignored or labeled as "one of those Bible-believing Christians." For some of us, I'm afraid, "persecution" is having the pastor tell us that our pet conviction or ministry in the church is not going to be the tail that wags the whole dog, subsequently causing us to shake the dust off our feet as we exit this church in search of another one...a "true church."

We are as spoiled as we are egocentric. We've never suffered any real hardships. We're not being beaten, tortured, or thrown into prison because of our religious beliefs. The closest we come to suffering, as a Christian subculture, is having some late-night comic make fun of our favorite televangelist.

The majority of believers in the Western Church hold to the belief that, should persecution threaten us, God will intervene and spare us. This stems from the deep-seated conviction that we are somehow God's favorites, and that, as such, we are immune from these atrocities. Perhaps this has begun to change a little in the wake of the September 11th attacks.

In some measure, this attitude that we are special and will be specially exempt from suffering is due to ignorance of God's Word. For others, it is the result of a false teaching that is rampant in some parts of the Church that says, "Suffering comes because of a lack of faith, or because we have allowed the enemy to have his way."

THE CHURCH AND PERSECUTION

When Jesus was asked about the signs of His second coming, He made it abundantly clear that certain things would befall all believers before His return prior to the end of the age. These included: tribulation, death, and being hated by all nations for His name's sake.

We would all do well to listen to what the Spirit says in Revelation to the church in Smyrna, because persecutions certainly befell the believers there. And so there is a message here for us all today.

In His letter, Jesus introduces Himself to these suffering saints as "the first and the last, who was dead, and has come to life" (Rev. 2:8b). Jesus is able to identify with these believers because He also has suffered, even to the point of death.

Addressing these believers, Jesus reminds them that He is aware of their tribulation and poverty (see Rev. 2:9). Please note: He never condemns them for their lack of faith. Imagine sending one of our Christian leaders to report on this particular church—I mean one who has bought into the notion that God always only wants to bless us with the good things of this world, the "gospel of health and prosperity." There is no question in my mind that these poor believers would be severely criticized for their lack of faith, not only regarding the way the enemy was kicking them around, but also because of their poverty.

Following that would come a good and lively exhortation based on the text, "You have not because you ask not," or some such promise. If you're tempted to throw this book down in anger, you especially need to read what the Spirit is saying to the Church today. In many parts of the Church we really have no theology regarding suffering or persecution. Throughout Church history there have been what we might call "poverty movements," that is, movements that reignited believers' devotion to living a simple life without focusing on accruing worldly possessions, in order to free themselves to serve Christ. These movements have always tried to mimic the early Church, in which believers sold their personal belongings and lived communally, sharing all things in common. I'm afraid that even to suggest starting such a movement today is tantamount to heresy...and people who do so are suspected of being "communists" or "cultists."

Forsaking the lure of worldly luxuries and goods, like experiencing persecution, has been the *norm* for many believers throughout the centuries. It still is the norm in much of the world outside the West.

FALSE CONCLUSIONS

Here in the West, I'm afraid, we're apt to look at a situation, in which we are relatively free of religious persecution, and come to some wrong conclusions.

First, we interpret the absence of persecution as if this is to be our permanent state. This is a big mistake, for which we could well pay dearly in the long run. The psalmist makes clear in Psalm chapter 2, that the nations are going to be in an uproar along with their kings and ruler. Together, they are going to arise against the Lord and His people, saying, "Let us tear their fetters apart and cast away their cords from us!" (Ps. 2:3) Fetters and cords are those things that restrain and hold things together.

The world hates the restraining influence of God's people. We seek to restrain movements in our culture that degrade humanity. The world insists it desires "freedom," so that everyone can do what's right in their own eyes without being told it's wrong. The world's longing is to rid itself of the Church's "light" in order to give free reign to deeds of darkness. I believe there is also in this world a sick and incipient hatred for God's first chosen people—the Jews. In fact, I personally believe we are going to see an increase of anti-Semitism, giving rise to worldwide hatred of all those who seek to aid the Jews.

I believe the Spirit is still speaking to the Church as a whole, reminding us to prepare ourselves for persecution as we engage in cultural wars we must wage to be the Church. Also we must prepare ourselves for the specially focused persecution that will be directed at us as we stand up for God's causes and for all His people. May we not dismiss this warning: It is not a matter of *if persecution will come*; it is only a matter of time as to when it will come.

NONETHELESS, WE ARE RICH AND AT PEACE

The beauty of these letters to each church is that they help us look beneath surface matters to see things as they appear to Christ in the Spirit. After observing their outward tribulation and poverty, He says, "...but you are rich" (Rev. 2:9a).

I'm guessing that nobody else ever would have drawn that conclusion about the believers in Smyrna. What Christ is seeing and revealing to us is that, for these believers, richness had nothing to do with owning stock or bonds, CDs, or mutual funds. Richness had to do with possessing spiritual character.

There is a subtle lesson here that we must not miss. The lesson, I believe, is that when times are easy we tend to get lax in our faith, and then we gravitate toward all the wonderful luxuries and trinkets the world has for sale. The problem is, as we buy into the world's offerings we pay more than cash...we pay at the expense of our souls. Trusting in outward things will always weaken spiritual character.

Only under the pressure of hardship and persecution, are we reminded of the world's shallowness and the deception of its promises. Only under pressure are we reminded that what is of real lasting value is that which is of the spirit. And it is no coincidence that, only under pressure is the real fragrance of

Christ—the spiritual character that is released from within us—made manifest.

On this matter, my father would often quote D. Martyn Lloyd-Jones, who said, "God's great concern for us primarily is not our happiness but our holiness."[2]

WE NEED TO BE "SIFTED"...EVERY ONE OF US

I enjoy watching people's reactions when I share a sort of homey version of an episode from the life of the apostle Peter in Luke chapter 22. I like to share it using my own words because it can help us all enter into the story ourselves. In this case, the Lord is speaking to Peter about some work that needs to be done in Peter's spirit, which is likely to be unpleasant.

Peter comes out for breakfast early one morning to find Jesus all alone. Peter asks the Lord, "Did you hear someone knocking very early this morning—before sunrise?"

Jesus says, "Yes, I did. I was up praying before daybreak, and I heard the knocking."

Peter asks, "Lord, who was knocking?"

Jesus says, "This may surprise you, but it was the devil."

"The devil!?" Peter exclaims. "Come on, Lord, don't joke with me like that."

Jesus replies, "I'm not joking. I'm telling you the truth."

"Lord," Peter asks in astonishment, "what did he want?"

"Actually, he came to talk to me about you," says Jesus.

"Oh, I get it," Peter smiles. "This is a joke."

"No," says Jesus evenly. "It's no joke. He came to ask my permission to sift your soul...the way wheat is sifted."

Peter startles, thinking of the violent, threshing motion used to separate the good kernels of wheat from the useless stem.

"Well if that's the case, Lord, am I ever glad You answered the door—uh, by the way...what exactly did you tell him?"

"I said, 'Go ahead. You have my permission.' "

"You what?!"

"I gave him permission. And I did it because I know that ultimately it won't destroy you or your faith. I know that in the outcome it will make you a seasoned man of God. For only when the useless chaff is taken out of your life will you be able to help others. And by the way, Peter, I know that you will not be destroyed and that your faith won't fail, because I Myself will be praying for you the whole time you are being sifted."

Most of us, I dare say, don't know this Jesus. The Jesus we know—that is, the one we have created in our minds—is the one who is ever ready to keep us from experiencing problems, the one who wants to shower us continually with the material blessings we long for. Yes, we have created a mental idol, an impostor, a "false Jesus" who wants us happy at all costs.

This is not the Jesus who is speaking to the suffering saints of Smyrna. Here we find the true Jesus, well aware of their present circumstances, and also well aware that a future furnace of affliction is coming.

"Do not fear what you are about to suffer," the Lord tells them (Rev. 2:10a). Notice that the Lord doesn't promise to intervene and wrest them from the clutches of their circumstances. He rather warns them that the crucible of testing they are in is about to be turned up to high. The devil, he says, is going to have them imprisoned and they will undergo a period of tribulation resulting in death. Like Peter, like each of us, the Smyrnans must undergo sifting.

OUR OWN GOSPEL

The very concept of being tried and tested so that we might learn how to let go of worldliness is not the clause we noticed when we accepted the "good news." This, of course, raises the question: Which version of the good news did we hear and accept? Was it the whole, true message Jesus delivered? Or the heavily edited one our Western Church culture offered to us, to get us to buy into a church membership?

The gospel of Jesus Christ, when it is declared in its entirety, tells us plainly that the only way to enter the Kingdom of God is through the doorway of suffering and letting go of self and its agendas. But I am afraid that this spiritual principle is so repulsive to most of us Westerners that we conveniently detour our way around it, seeking to avoid it at all cost. In its place, we substitute our own gospel of health, wealth, and pleasure.

If we ignore this letter to the church at Smyrna, and what it saying to all of us today, we do so at great peril to our souls. If we do so, we rob the message of the gospel of its true power in our lives. The church at Smyrna—poor, persecuted, and headed for even more persecution—is one of the few churches that had no need of repentance. Jesus has no words of condemnation for them, just the encouragement to remain faithful unto death. Jesus has the same words of encouragement for each one of us, as we suffer persecution, and also as we struggle against the force within us that resists dying the spiritual death to ourselves we must each die if we are going to enter into and live in the Kingdom of God.

Does this sound "old hat" to you? Does the more contemporary "gospel of blessing" appeal to your taste? I am going to be so bold as to suggest that you should distrust your tastes.

As a teacher in the Body of Christ I often find myself at odds with the latest trends. Let me say emphatically that I believe we have not even begun to see all that the Lord has for His people. Like Paul, I too press on that I may know Him (see Phil. 3:10). There is, however, a widespread belief that somehow if we can only "take hold" of God, and find some ultimate, bottom-line principle by which God wants us to live, then we can arrive at some type of Christian "Nirvana." Nothing else will be asked of us; we'll be at leisure, and we will simply drink in the cool refreshing waters of His presence. While this type of preaching generates great excitement and draws large crowds, it is a far cry from what the Scriptures teach.

Take Paul's life as an example. For every "trip to Heaven" he made—and there is only one that we are told of—he encountered numerous other experiences of suffering. Just read his list in Second Corinthians 11:23-28, where Paul lists his experiences: "...in far more labors, in far more imprisonments, beaten times without number, often in danger of death...." Following this we have an almost unbelievable list of even more dangers that faced Paul.

Don't get me wrong. We need times when we are at rest in the presence of our first love—and we must remember that the Ephesians were counseled to seek Christ's living presence. Personally, I long for more of the manifest presence of God. But I'm also aware that many Christians make the mistake of seeking some sort of interior tranquility rather than seeking Christ.

And there is a huge difference. In one case, "inner peace" becomes God; in the other case Christ remains God.

Oftentimes, it is through the experiences of suffering that we discover the presence of God with us. After all, it was while John was imprisoned on the Isle of Patmos as a "fellow partaker in the tribulation" (see Rev. 1:9) that he received this amazing revelation of the Lord.

In the end, a gospel that denies or ignores God's purposes in our suffering is not the true gospel, but one of our own invention.

VALUING WHAT CHRIST VALUES

Ultimately, what this letter to the Smyrnans gives us is one more aspect of the spiritual character Jesus Christ values in His people. It is of great importance for us to value what Jesus Christ values because it is the standard that is going to be applied to us as we are "sifted" by trial and lack in this life.

Faithfulness is the cardinal virtue for which the church at Smyrna is commended. Here are a people that have suffered the loss of their homes and possessions, undergone rejections, blasphemies, and tribulation, and yet have remained steadfast through it all. They have experienced firsthand what it is to walk through the valley of the shadow of death and have come through victoriously. Unlike their Ephesian brothers and sisters, they have maintained their first love despite adverse circumstances.

And what the Spirit shows us is a wonderful glimpse of Jesus Christ, standing on the sidelines, encouraging them to keep going, letting them know that the finish line is fast approaching and soon they will cross it if they will just remain faithful (see Rev. 2:10). The Spirit is offering the same powerful encouragement to us today: Be faithful to the end.

I have heard it said that a faithful man is to be preferred any day to a gifted man. Giftedness certainly speaks of God's generosity...but it may have little to do with character of the person in whom the gift rests. We all know gifted charlatans and immoral people. Faithfulness, however, is a quality that can only come out of godly character. One day every believer will stand before the judgment seat of Christ where every work will be examined as to its eternal value. Those whose works are approved because they reflected the brilliant character of Christ to a dark world will hear these words, "Well done, good and faithful servant" (Mt. 25:21a NKJV)!

If we want to value what Christ tells us to value, then in our lives faithfulness must be held in greater esteem than successfulness. Time after time throughout the New Testament, we find this word *faithful* used. Moses was said to be faithful over his house (see Heb. 3:5). Paul refers to himself this way in writing to Timothy: "I thank Christ Jesus our Lord, who has strengthened me, because he considered me faithful..." (1 Tim. 1:12a). Paul admonished Timothy to pour into the lives of faithful men the things that he himself had been taught, so that they in turn would teach other faithful men the same things (see 2 Tim. 2:2). Onesimus is referred to as "our faithful and beloved brother" (see Col. 4:9a), as were many other brethren.

Is it dawning on us yet that neither riches, nor the size of a church or ministry, are ever used as gauges by which God approves a spiritual leader or his work?

I have no doubt that one day we are going to be shocked at the rewards that will be handed out to brothers and sisters in Christ who, in the world's eyes, appeared to do little, and yet

God saw their faithfulness. I, for one, will be humbled to be in the company of these dear saints of Smyrna and many others since, who have triumphed in tribulation and persecution. These are the experiences that produce mature and strong saints.

I learned recently that scientists working in the "biosphere dome" were surprised to find that the trees were not growing tall and straight, but rather were bending over. They came to the conclusion that it was because there were no winds or storms. They had produced the perfect environment, yet it failed to produce healthy trees. Without adversity, these trees grew quickly at first, but in the end they had no strength to stand tall. Herein lies a warning for the present-day Western Church.

Christianity Today recently published the following article on the persecuted Church. In closing this chapter, I offer here an excerpt that can speak to all of us:

> To the angel of the church of the despised, incarcerated, separated, raped, and martyred; the persecuted Church. These are the words of him who knows your patient endurance, understands your distress, and like you has been faithful to the shedding of his blood.
>
> You say you are isolated, cut off, that no one acknowledges your state. I see the terrors you face: the raids of your house churches in Laos, Indonesia, and China; the assault and murder of your leadership in Iran, India, and Chechnya; the indiscriminate bombing and enslavement that ravage your villages in Sudan.
>
> I register every tear that is cried, record each longing conceived, hear each desperate plea confessed. I

identify intimately with your plight. I have not forgotten you. Nor have many others who, although unfamiliar with the gravity of your suffering, draw hope and strength from your noble sacrifices for me. I have revealed your plight to your brothers and sisters in Christ and have called thousands of churches to pray for you and serve you....

Beware of those who come from outside your fellowship, who masquerade as teachers of the church but elevate personal comfort over godly obedience. Many travel from long distances and present themselves as spiritual masters of the faith, proclaiming that temporal health and security are your due. Do not listen to them. Theirs is a false teaching, only shackling you to the unrequited masters of greed and disquiet. In the midst of your suffering, I will prove to be your true peace and anchor....

I delight in your resourcefulness with little, your dignity in suffering, your joyful endurance in the midst of adversity. It is these things that give witness to a power above all earthly kingdoms, a source of strength stronger than the might of any human power.

Remain faithful, and I will raise you up in victory. Patiently endure, for I will not tarry long.[3]

ENDNOTES

1. Paul Marshall, *Their Blood Cries Out* (Dallas, TX: Word Publishers, 1997), p. 4.

2. D. Martyn Lloyd-Jones, *Spiritual Depression: Its Causes and Cures* (London: Pickering & Inglis, Ltd., n.d.), p. 235.

3. See the October 25, 1999 issue, p. 73, for the full article.

CHAPTER 10

PERGAMUM—THE COMPROMISING CHURCH

SO FAR WE ARE LEARNING a number of things about standards by which Christ evaluates His churches and the works of those of us who are leading and building His Church. We cannot lose sight of the reason why this study is so urgent: I, for one, don't want to stand before Him one day and have to say, "Lord, I didn't know You felt that strongly about those matters. I thought it would please You if I did these great exploits. See? Aren't they wonderful? Didn't I do great things in Your name?"

In that day, the Lord will cut swiftly to the core of the matter with us, revealing what our true motive was all along. Therefore, it is important to listen to what the Spirit is saying about the true nature of our work for Him, lest we be shocked and disappointed in that final day when the truth about our innermost motive is brought to light.

SOMETHING ROTTEN AT THE CORE

What can we learn from the Spirit's letter to the church at Pergamum?

None of these letters ramble on about trivial things, do they? Each one goes right to the heart of the matter. How often we "strain at gnats and swallow camels" (see Mt. 23:24b). Here, the color of the choir robes or the type of seating is never the issue.

From the outset, it obviously centers around two problems going on within the Church about which Jesus is deeply concerned. The real issue here revolves around the teaching of Balaam and the teaching of the Nicolaitans.

Now most of us have never thought much about Balaam. As to his teachings, few of us even have a clue what they are. We have three references in the New Testament to this Old Testament prophet—four if you include Paul's reference to the "fruit" of Balaam's counsel (see 1 Cor. 10:7-8). The first reference is found in Second Peter where it talks about the "*way of Balaam*" (see 2 Pet. 2:15). The second, in Jude's epistle, speaks of the "*error* of Balaam" (see Jude 11). And finally, here in the letter to the Pergamum church, we have a negative reference to "the *teaching* of Balaam" (see Rev. 2:14).

Even a casual glance at the order of these three references reveals that there is a progression of thought. We begin with "the way"; this leads to "the error," which in turn becomes "the teaching."

BALAAM, AND THE WAY OF BALAAM

Who is this man, Balaam? We are first introduced to him in Numbers 22.

Israel, God's people, had travelled from Egypt and were now camped in the plains of Moab opposite Jericho. The king of Moab was a man called Balak. Balak had been keeping track of Israel's movements and had learned what they had done to the Amorites. Balak, along with his people, were terrified of Israel and sought to have them cursed.

Enter Balaam. Balaam was known for his prophetic gifting, and he was called upon by Balak to curse Israel. Interestingly, Balaam's name means "swallower of people." Balak wanted to have Balaam curse Israel so that they would become weak. Then Balak would attack them and drive them out. He knew that because of Israel's size, he had no way of defeating them unless they were first cursed. So he dispatched his elders to visit Balaam with a proposal: If Balaam would curse Israel, he would be rewarded financially.

When Balaam heard the offer, he sought the mind of God. In no uncertain terms he was told not to go with Balak's elders and not to curse Israel because God had placed His blessing upon them.

When Balak was informed of Balaam's answer, he sent a second delegation, with an even better offer. They pleaded with Balaam to accept the offer and begged him not to delay. Once again he was told that he would be honored richly for his "ministry." It is apparent from this passage that Balak's men had found Balaam's Achilles' heel—the love of money. At first, Balaam put on a brave front, saying no amount of money would allow him to go contrary to God's command. But he detained the men for the night, saying he needed to pray about the situation.

In the end, God gave him permission to go, but only because of Balaam's insistence—and it is clear that God was angry with him for going. This is what I believe Peter was referring to when he referred to "the way of Balaam." Balaam typifies all of us who wheedle and pressure God, all the while rationalizing what it is we want to do to give in to compromise. We go "our way" as opposed to God's way. And how often God permits us to have our way—but the "end is the way of death" (Prov. 14:12b).

From here, many of us recall the story. As Balaam rides on his donkey to deliver his message to Balak, the angel of the Lord stands before him blocking his path. Eventually Balaam's eyes are opened and he sees the angel before him. God speaks to him and says, "Behold, I have come out as an adversary, because *your way* was contrary to Me" (Num. 22:32b).

Please note: When our way is contrary to God's revealed will, we too are heading in the "*way* of Balaam." And unfortunately, this is not the end of the matter.

THE ERROR OF BALAAM

The way of Balaam, as noted earlier, gives place to the error of Balaam.

The word *error* used here is the Greek word for "delusion, deception, fraudulence, to wander." Balaam's insistence on having his own way opened him to deception and error.

Paul warns that every one of us is susceptible to wandering from the truth. Consider his grave warning to the Thessalonians: "...because they did not receive the love of the truth [God's way] so as to be saved. For this reason God will send upon them a deluding influence so that they will believe what is false [follow an erroneous line of reasoning]" (2 Thess. 2:10b-11).

Balaam had allowed himself to follow a false line of reasoning. He did so because he wanted the huge purse of money they were offering him. And so from one statement the Lord made to him—approval to go with the Moabites—he followed false reasoning until he had deceived himself into thinking that perhaps God wouldn't mind so much after all if he cursed the people of Israel.

THE TEACHING OF BALAAM

The mercy of God in this story is amazing. Balaam is given several chances to repent. Balak on three separate occasions takes Balaam to curse Israel. Each time, God speaks words of blessing upon them, refusing Balaam permission to curse them. Balak is furious and says to Balaam, "I said I would honor you greatly, but behold, the Lord has held you back from honor" (Num. 24:11b). Balaam returns to his home—but not before he makes a final grave mistake.

Balaam's love for money is quite apparently devouring his soul by now. He simply must have it. Because God has repeatedly blessed Israel, Balaam's mind goes into overdrive, and he devises a teaching that spreads through Israel, causing the whole nation to sin greatly so that God Himself will curse them. This diabolical plan is later revealed in Numbers 31:16, where we are told that he counsels Balak and the elders of Moab how they can corrupt God's people through idolatry and immorality, insuring that God would judge Israel.

It is clear that Balaam's teaching is indeed spread, like contagion, throughout Israel. The end result of his counsel is seen in Numbers 25, where we find God's people mingling with the daughters of Moab. The Moabite women extend an invitation to the men of Israel to join them for a time of feasting and celebration. Although we are not told this in Numbers, the psalmist adds this information in Psalm 106:28: "They joined themselves also to Baal-peor, and ate sacrifices offered to the dead."

As the teaching of Balaam corrupts Israel, the people of God violate God's call to separation, and they freely mix with the heathens, not only worshiping their gods, but also conceiving children with them. When God sees this blatant display of idolatry and immorality, He releases judgment, and some 24,000 men die in the plague.

What was the teaching of Balaam? It revolved around the idea that because they were the blessed covenant people of God, they could not be cursed. G. Campbell Morgan makes this comment: "The doctrine of Balaam broadly stated was, undoubtedly, that seeing that they were the covenant people of God, they might with safety indulge themselves in social intercourse with their neighbors for no harm could happen to them."[1]

It appears that in order to mislead Israel, Balaam informs them that God will not allow him to curse them. The reason, he said, is because God has blessed them. Therefore, because of this covenant of blessing they have no need to fear any judgment with regards to their conduct.

The false security this gives the Israelites then becomes the basis for their accepting the Moabites' offer to join with them in their sexual perversion and idolatry.

Paul, writing to the Corinthian believers, cites this specific episode in Israel's history as being one of the reasons they failed to enter the promised land. He then adds, "Now these things happened to them as an example, and they were written for our instruction, upon whom the ends of the age have come. Therefore let him who thinks he stands take heed that he does not fall" (1 Cor. 10:11-12).

PERGAMUM...AND US

It is interesting to me that so little attention is given to this "teaching of Balaam" and its relevance to the Body of Christ today. In some sectors of the Church we hear a great deal about the "Jezebel spirit" and her influence today. And yet, at best, we have only two references to Jezebel—one passage in the Old Testament and one here in Revelation—and nobody can say for sure that there is any correlation between them. Why is it then, that when we have four references in the New Testament to the spiritually corrosive and disastrous effect of Balaam's teaching upon Israel, we place such little importance upon it?

Let us seriously consider Balaam's teaching, in light of the fact that the same Spirit that issued a warning against it to the church at Pergamum is warning us to beware this false line of reasoning today.

Balaam began to leave the way of the Lord when he was dazzled by the promise of wealth, and the taste of all the world's goods he had ever wanted remained on his tongue. Jesus warns us about "the deceitfulness of riches" (see Mt. 13:22). Importantly, out of all seven churches Pergamum was perhaps the wealthiest city of them all. It is here, among worldly riches, that we find satan's throne and seat of power. Truly the love of money is the root of all sorts of evil (see 1 Tim. 6:10). Balaam's teaching took hold in the church at Pergamum because here were a people within the Body of Christ who allowed themselves to be deceived. Their deception stemmed from the thinking that their wealth was a sign of God's blessing. Moreover, because they were under blessing and not judgment, God was not concerned about how they lived.

J.B. Stoney, in his wonderful series entitled *Ministry*, says this with regard to the evil and misleading way of Balaam:

> Amalek was Satan's power to prevent you from leaving the world. The device of Balaam is to prevent your entering the land...Satan now would minister

to the susceptibility of your nature. This device begins by the invitation, not an opposition now, but a
solicitation—an offer to gratify you where naturally
you can be most gratified... Thus Balaam succeeds
by ministering to the most vital part of one's nature.[2]

Stoney also writes:

...there is a [second] force against you, and that is
Balaam. Balaam represents the tactics of the enemy
to get the people into social intercourse, and he did
them more mischief than any other form of satanic
opposition. So it is in this day. The Balaam snare is
the masterpiece of satanic wickedness for the people
of God. Nothing has corrupted us as much as company. It is the society that Christians keep that does
the mischief. And mark my words! Every one is col-
ored by the lowest company that he keeps."[3]

Today, as in ancient Israel and Pergamum, we are so willing to be convinced by spiritual leaders that we can mingle with
the world and come out unscathed. The Scriptures speak contrary to this. Listen to the psalmist:

They did not destroy the peoples, as the Lord commanded
them, but they mingled with the nations and learned their
practices, and served their idols, which became a snare to
them. They even sacrificed their sons and their daughters to
the demons and shed innocent blood, the blood of their sons
and their daughters...whom they sacrificed to the idols of
Canaan; and the land was polluted with the blood. Thus
they became unclean in their practices, and played the har-
lot in their deeds (Psalm 106:34-39).

Most of us would abhor the thought of this type of involvement because we, today, no longer have these pagan festivals with their overtly devilish practices. The apostle James, however, saw it differently, when he wrote, "...know ye not that the friendship of the world is enmity with God?" (Jas. 4:4a KJV). In our friendship with the world, are we not being absorbed by the world, when we allow our children's spirits to be consumed by the demonic lyrics in the music they listen to? Or when we come up with lines of reasoning to condone sacrificing children on the altar of convenience through abortion?

The modern-day Church is as friendly with the world today as she has ever been. We have mingled closely; and the world's ways, its errors, and its lines of reasoning have too frequently become our own.

"ONCE BLESSED, NEVER CURSED"?

Before ending this chapter, I want to return to another important aspect of this "teaching of Balaam." It would appear from the text that the teachings of the Nicolaitans are also grouped together here with that of Balaam.

G. Campbell Morgan refers to it as "...the perilous and damnable heresy that sin cannot violate a covenant." He continues, "...the heresy which has come to be known in later days as the Antinomian heresy, the heresy which says, you are safe in the Name and in the faith, that it matters little about your conduct. You may mix with the sinners of Pergamum [the world] and follow their habits and yet share the benefits of the covenant."[4]

This is where I am likely to offend all my Baptist and Calvanistic brothers, though I hope I will not. But I know of no better modern equivalent in the Church world today that parallels the teaching of Balaam than that of the doctrine of eternal security—or as it is popularly stated, "once saved, always saved" or "once blessed and you will never again come under the curse."

I want to pose this very serious question for us all to consider: Is it possible that this teaching is leading souls to destruction, and possibly even to hell?

Today we have hundreds of thousands of *believers* who are convinced that they can mingle with the world, engage in immorality and every other sin...and yet still retain their salvation. In the Church we have epidemic divorce—at a rate higher than that of the world at large. It is interesting to note that according to the late Donald Grey Barnhouse, the name Pergamos has the same root from which we get our English words for bigamy and polygamy.[5]

Another commentator and scholar states,

> [Pergamos is connected to] the word for marriage. The particle which forms the first syllable frequently calls attention to something that is objectionable. *Pergamos* signifies a mixed marriage in the most objectionable sense of the word, for it is the marriage of the organization of the Church of Jesus Christ with the world.[6]

Israel's union with the Moabites cost them the lives of some 24,000 of their own. This judgment shows the extent of God's anger against *mixture* of any kind. No wonder, then, that we have four references to Balaam and his actions in the New Testament. Yet why is it that we hear so little teaching regarding this major event in Israel's history? I believe one reason is that it has become far more popular to blame some "spirit" (Jezebel) than it is to deal with the works of the flesh. Like Adam, our forefather, we're quick to blame somebody else (Eve), rather than acknowledge our own sinful condition.

Jesus warns the church in Pergamum that unless they repent from following the teaching of Balaam He will make war against them with the sword of His mouth. Looking back at God's anger against Israel in the incident at Baal of Peor, we discover that after their sin with the Moabites God told Moses to execute the leaders, and these men perished by the sword. This may also have reference to the actions of Phinehas who during Israel's harlotry with the daughters of Moab rose up with his sword/spear to execute judgment on an Israelite. This Israelite had blatantly taken a Moabite woman into his tent while Moses and the rest of the congregation looked on, in order to engage in immorality with her. Phinehas ran his sword through both of them and brought the plague to an end. God in turn praised Phinehas for his actions and bestowed on him a "perpetual priesthood"—"because he was jealous for his God" (Num. 25:1-13).

Here we see the great high priest, the Lord Jesus Christ, promising to wage war against his church unless they turn and repent of their way—idolatry and immorality. God was not going to physically kill the leaders of the church at Pergamum, but He was going to smite them in spirit by the awesome power of His Word.

Likewise, God will do the same with His Church in the present. We hear a great deal today regarding spiritual warfare and assume that the greatest power that can oppose the Church, and us as believers, is satan and his minions. That is not the case. In Revelation we see a picture of the God who is willing to go to war with His Church if that is what it takes to turn her back from evil ways, error, and insidious teachings that are destroying her. Just as God sent fiery serpents into the camp of Israel, so He warns the Church, both yesterday and today, that He will not tolerate the teachings of Balaam. Judgment begins at the house of God (see 1 Pet. 4:17).

CONCLUSION

We can no longer afford to let the ways of the world infect us.

ENDNOTES

1. G. Campbell Morgan, *The Letters of Our Lord* (London: Pickering & Inglis, Ltd., n.d.), p. 51.

2. J.B. Stoney, *Ministry, Vol. 12* (Lancing, Sussex, BN159LX, England: Kingston Bible Trust, N.D.), pp. 393-394.

3. J.B. Stoney, *Ministry, Vol. 6* (Lancing, Sussex, BN159LX, England: Kingston Bible Trust, N.D.), p. 331.

4. Morgan, p. 51.

5. Lehman Strauss, *The Book of Revelation* (Neptune, NJ: Loizeaux Brothers, Inc., 1977), p. 54.

6. *Ibid.*

CHAPTER 11

THYATIRA—THE "TOLERANT" CHURCH

Recently, I witnessed an incredible devastation—a church torn apart. It came about because one man, a so-called "prophet," went on what can only be called a "witch hunt."

The hunt began when this man began singling out those in the church who had strong personalities. Not too surprisingly, the ones he focused upon especially were women over whom he had no control. Not that these were necessarily resistant or sinful women. But they were not to be manipulated. In hindsight, one can see how this man's frustration level rose over time, until tragically, the tension moved from the human plane, where things might have been talked out, to the supernatural plane. This mistake occurred when the man began to use a phrase, and an accusation that has become all too common in some sectors of the Church today. He began to point the finger at these women, claiming they had "the spirit of Jezebel."

In short order, the church was decimated.

I believe there has been immeasurable harm done to the Body of Christ today, and it has occurred because the word "controlling" has been applied to certain members. I have witnessed firsthand the devastation caused by those pointing the finger of accusation at a brother or sister, labeling them as having a *Jezebel spirit.*

It is high time we stopped the devastation and took a hard look at what is going on here.

JEZEBEL REVISITED

Jezebel. After almost three millennia this long neglected character from the past has enjoyed a resurgence of popularity in recent years. Her reputation has spread around the Church world, and if she were as half as magnetic to the secular press as she is in the Church her picture would be on the cover of every leading magazine. What is it about this woman Jezebel that has the Christian world in such a frenzy? What has elevated her to her current status as the "queen of principalities"?

In some parts of the Church, "the Jezebel spirit" has become the favorite scapegoat and is blamed for whatever problems are troubling the flock. To some, her power and influence are almost greater than the devil himself.

Here in the second chapter of Revelation, as the Spirit addresses the church at Thyatira, there is indeed serious concern about the influence of "the woman Jezebel" (see Rev. 2: 20). Let us examine the matter carefully and separate fact from fiction.

THE FACTS

First, we need to understand that Jezebel did not have total sway over the congregation at Thyatira. She did not control everything that went on in the church. It is important to understand that her alleged power and position have greatly evolved over the centuries. How do we know? Because Jesus begins by commending these believers for their love, faith, service, and perseverance. This was the only church of the seven that received a commendation for its love. This divine endorsement tells us that this was a church deeply devoted to its Lover and Master. They were free from the love of pleasure, money, and self; and had maintained a deep affection for Christ.

My friend Mike Bickle, founder of the Metro Christian Fellowship in Kansas City, talks about the three faces of Jesus in the Book of Revelation: the affectionate Bridegroom; the glorious sovereign King; and the fierce righteous Judge. In his opening remarks, as we see, Jesus appears to the church in Thyatira as the affectionate Bridegroom, responding to His affectionate Bride.

We know from this that, despite something amiss in their church, these were a people who maintained their passion and purity. It is important to keep these facts in mind as we consider the influence of this woman, because too many Christian writers and teachers have elevated her to a position of greater power and authority than the believers themselves. One would almost think that any woman with a powerful presence operating in a local congregation today would certainly bring about its demise. This is not an accurate or fair account of how the Scriptures reveal the real Jezebel.

And that is just our first mistake.

The second mistake is to make a wrong connection between this Jezebel and another notorious woman from the Old Testament—Jezebel, the wife of King Ahab.

I want to point out a common mistake that's often made when studying the Scriptures. We need to be careful that we don't jump to conclusions with regard to other passages of Scripture that appear to have similarities, but in fact may have no relationship at all. For example, we don't study the life of Saul in the Old Testament to gain added insight into the Saul of the New Testament. Nor do we study the life of Joseph who became ruler of Egypt in order to learn something about Joseph, the husband of Mary. And yet, many modern teachers study Jezebel, the evil, conniving wife of Ahab and connect her with the woman Jezebel, who Scripture refers to as a "prophetess" in Thyatira (see Rev. 2: 20). The Scriptures apparently didn't.

The third mistake I believe we make in terms of the Thyatiran's Jezebel is that we have added a supernatural dimension to her where none exists. We now hear about "the spirit of Jezebel." One thing I've noticed after 39 years of ministry—as soon as you put the word *spirit* before something it immediately adds thrill value to its appeal. The Bible never addresses this woman as the "*Jezebel spirit.*" Using this term may boost the sale of tapes, or increase our insatiable hunger to know more about this evil wonder-woman; but alas, the Word of God does not bestow this title or any such power upon her.

And what do we make of the fact that the Lord Himself "gave [Jezebel] time to repent" (see Rev. 2:21)? If we assume that some major *spirit* was residing in this woman, then instead of giving her time to repent, wouldn't the Lord have instructed the church to call for a time of prayer and fasting in order to cast out this monster? I've never heard of repentance being used to exorcise a spirit.

Don't misunderstand me. It does appear that this woman was deceived and she was involved in spreading false teaching. I'm sure the enemy was using her *big time*, for certainly her teaching was not given through the inspiration of the Spirit of

God. What we do know about this woman is that she was self-appointed and self-anointed. She had given herself the title of "prophetess" and, in turn, gathered about her a group of ardent followers. This little band of disciples were eager to follow her every revelation and teaching. And apparently her message of "liberty" gave them the license they were looking for.

Before we go any further, allow me to address the prophetic role. I firmly believe that the Church is suffering due to the great lack of the prophetic ministry, whether in the exercise of the gift or that of the prophetic office. The prophetic office is an essential part of the ministry used for the equipping of the saints. We neglect it at our own peril. Paul clearly expressed the need for the "fivefold ministry," saying they were given to the church "until we all attain to the unity of the faith...to a mature man" (see Eph. 4:11-13).

One thing is clear from Scripture and that is these fivefold ministers work together; never in isolation, as was the case with Jezebel. Whenever you find a person working alone and not in association with others, this should signal an immediate alarm. We have in Acts the statement that there were in the church at Antioch "prophets and teachers." This provides balance, accountability, and the necessary confirmation of which the Scriptures speak: "...by the mouth of two or three witnesses every fact may be confirmed" (Mt. 18:16). The voice of the Lone Ranger is a dangerous voice to follow.

Today's Church needs be aware of the dangers of those working in isolation, especially as it relates to prophetic ministry.

FALSE TEACHING

Jezebel had not only set herself up as a prophetess; she had also stepped into the role of teacher. It has been my experience over the past 39 years of ministry that you seldom find someone who is used in a strong prophetic gifting, also functioning in a teaching capacity. (There are exceptions, of course.) I believe there is a reason why this is so.

Those who function the best in the prophetic are usually those who belong to a team ministry. One of the great needs in the Body of Christ is the marriage of the Spirit with the word of God. Jesus said, "You are mistaken, not understanding the Scriptures nor the power of God" (Mt. 22:29b). Those who function mainly in the Spirit need to be linked with those who function in the word and vice versa.

This is because prophetic ministry, by its very nature, is somewhat mystical. Therefore it needs to be examined carefully by the "more sure word of prophecy." I believe much prophetic ministry is rejected due to a lack of understanding what I call *the anatomy of the prophetic word*. (More on that in the next chapter.)

Jezebel not only taught but also led the people. No doubt her revelations set her apart as having special insight and therefore drew an eager group of devoted followers. It was this influence that has now earned her the dubious title of "the controlling spirit" or "Jezebel spirit." All leaders, good or bad, godly or ungodly, exercise a certain amount of influence or control; that is the very nature of a leader. The problem with Jezebel's influence was that it was contrary to God's Word and purpose.

Do you see the important point I'm getting at here? Jezebel's problem was not so much a "control problem." Rather, she had wandered off into wrong doctrines and had become a false teacher, leading others away from the knowledge of the truth. It would appear that her private revelations were ultimately taught as doctrines, which in turn were translated into action by those who became "doers of the word"—her word. What these private revelations were, we do not know. However, we do see the fruit of her teaching—immorality and idolatry.

The Scriptures show that Jezebel's attitude and teachings resulted in loose sexual behavior. Perhaps this stemmed from a wrong concept of grace, an overemphasis on the Father's love, or from some other teaching that minimized the standard of God's holiness.

Moreover, the Lord's response to this woman was not to set the church upon a witch hunt to see who had been "infected" by her spirit. His response was to give her time to repent of her immorality. Why have we overlooked this, and given Jezebel some kind of supernatural status, as being inhabited by a "spirit"?

I believe it is because the phrase that is used in Revelation in connection with Jezebel is that she has knowledge of "the deep things of satan" (see Rev. 2:24). But the question arises: Did she really have this knowledge—or only purport to have it? More likely, it was posturing. For it appears that some pretense at knowing the mysteries of the satanic realm was the drawing card of her ministry. But it was a false front, a mask of power, a way to deceive other people into respecting her. Again, excusing sin and leading others into immorality was her great sin.

OUR "PET SINS"—EXPOSED

We are living in a day when we, too, are easily drawn in and mesmerized by someone who claims to have supernatural knowledge, especially of the satanic realm. To put it plainly, we are suckers for a cheap thrill.

Consider the fact that the theme of spiritual warfare is currently as hot a topic as it has ever been. Not missions, mind you, but the seeking out and bringing down of "satanic strongholds." As I have studied this topic and read numerous books and articles, there appears to be a growing fascination among believers with "the deep things of satan." And if you pay attention to the teachings on this topic, every year spiritual warfare becomes more and more complex. The deeper we go into this arena, the more weird it all becomes. There is a strange and alluring quality to spiritual warfare, which causes those who major in it to be caught up in its "depths."

Due to my age, I have the unique opportunity to span two generations. I distinctly remember hearing for the first time terms like "spiritual mapping," " warfare banners," "warfare on high places," "identification repentance," "reconciliation movements," and numerous other concoctions. New terms have appeared, in fact, every few months. I recall when the Church was naïve enough to believe that the name of Jesus was sufficient to pull down strongholds. Now there is a ministry that spends tens of thousands of dollars hauling believers to some ancient "high place" in order to depose "the queen of heaven" or some newly discovered principality.

Where is all this "insight" into the weird and satanic really taking us? We go deeper and deeper into trying to unravel the enemy's ways and, in turn, become more and more intrigued with his *depths*. Every week someone produces a new tape or book, apparently vying for the title of *guru of spiritual warfare*. Sadly, I think it's possible that the enemy is reveling in all the attention, and that he may be the one who continues to provide *revelation* to those so desperate to stay ahead of the pack.

And all the while we are looking outside ourselves for the source of the problem, our own pet sins lie undiscovered and unexamined.

BACK TO THYATIRA...

If we return to sanity, and look with clear eyes at the Spirit's letter to Thyatira, what we see is that they tolerated a woman who taught false doctrine that led to immorality. Do we see what's happened here?

The sin for which this church was being corrected was having a tolerance for what should not have been tolerated.

If we consider what the Spirit is saying to us today through this letter, it is this: We, too, err when tolerance takes priority over holiness.

Why do we no longer hunger to hear messages against sin and ungodly living? Where are the voices in Christianity that we need to hear, proclaiming a message of holiness? Why do we hear messages about blessing and prosperity, or about self-improvement or some equally self-centered topic?

Yes, Jezebel is alive. But she is not some woman sitting on the end of the pew, manipulating others against the pastor and elders. Rather, the influence of Jezebel comes to us today through the so-called man of God standing in the pulpit proclaiming some watered-down version of the gospel that is devoid of the cross. He is the one who speaks of nothing concerning repentance and holy living, but rather stresses God's understanding of our "hang-ups" and "problems." He is the one who excuses our self-centered and carnal acts.

THE REAL JEZEBEL IN THE CHURCH

If we are going to invoke the name Jezebel, then at least let us be clear on what she was really known for. Control is never mentioned; manipulation is never mentioned; but *immorality* and *idolatry* are.

We would do well today to ask the Spirit to search our hearts, and to show us where we are tolerant of these attitudes that lead us away from God and into sin. This will take careful soul-searching, because today's idols are not the primitive works of art that our pagan forefathers bowed down to, but rather the sophisticated gods of sports, finance, pleasure, and sex. As well, the laxness in our morality will be harder to spot because we talk in terms of "understanding" and we think that tolerating all manner of things is a virtue. So while we in the Church are out hunting for the enemy that we might "wage spiritual warfare" against him, the enemy has silently infiltrated within us by breaching the walls of our own souls.

This is the real Jezebel—the spirit of tolerance and compromise, one we have allowed to infiltrate the Church rendering her impotent of all spiritual life, and diverting her energy into carnal pursuits, rather than advancing the Kingdom we are supposed to love.

I believe it was this spirit that another New Testament stalwart, Jude, was also trying to counter when he wrote his epistle. This beloved disciple of Christ was earnestly contending for the faith, which was once for all delivered to the saints, and which he saw eroding. What was Jude's concern? Certain men had crept in, unnoticed. They had gradually turned the grace of God into licentiousness.

William Barclay tells us these teachers promoted the idea that "all things belong to Christ, and therefore all things are his. And, therefore, for [us] there is nothing forbidden. So these heretics in Jude turn the grace of God into an excuse for flagrant and blatant immorality...."[1]

Today's "new attitudes" toward "winning people to Christ" are often nothing more than an attempt, really, to fill pews. We have repackaged God to our own liking. Our new God is forever wearing a happy face. He's more loving and understands our weaknesses and "hang-ups." We have given God this facelift because we are really actually afraid of offending people by calling sin, sin. But by softening our approach to morality and the idols of the day, we turn around and offend a holy God.

Herein lies our idolatry: This new, more "user friendly" god is far more interested in our happiness than our holiness. Riches are in; relationship is out. Holy passion for the things of God has been replaced by personal passion and fulfillment.

I want to warn you what will happen, though, if you repent and turn back to worshiping the one true God, to whom idolatry and immorality really do count as sin. Anyone teaching on discipline, holiness, or commitment is said to have a religious spirit. Whereas the Body of Christ should have no tolerance for sin, it now has little tolerance for talk about being separated from the world and becoming holy.

CONCLUSION

The Scriptures tell us that God searches our minds and hearts (see Rev. 2:23). The word translated as "hearts" literally means kidneys. The function of the kidneys in the natural body is that of filtering and eliminating waste from the body.

The Body of Christ in Thyatira was suffering from kidney failure. What should have been eliminated was allowed to remain within the body, poisoning it. And because of a lax and tolerant attitude, nobody seemed to notice or be concerned about the toxin. The Spirit said, "Wake up. Look at what's happening to you."

Today, we too need to heed the Spirit's warning. Body of Christ—we are allowing ourselves to be toxified by our tolerance of idolatry and immorality. We no longer expose sin and eliminate it by taking corrective action. Church discipline, rehabilitation, and restoration of sinners is a healthy process that has vanished into the dim past. Today, we do not know how to govern ourselves, and it is the spirit of holy self-discipline that the Spirit of God must restore if we are to be His holy and powerful witnesses in the earth. For how will we ever have authority with the world if we do not know how to govern ourselves?

This world must become "the Kingdom of our Lord and of His Christ..." (Rev. 11:15b). We, the servants of the Lord, are still tasked with working at His side to make it so. For this reason, the Spirit is still saying to the Church, "He who overcomes...to him I will give authority over the nations" (Rev. 2:26).

ENDNOTE

1. William Barclay, *The Letters of John and Jude* (Philadelphia: The Westminster Press, 1960), p. 217.

CHAPTER 12

SARDIS—THE "LIVE" CHURCH THAT IS DEAD

IF THERE IS ONE GREAT CENTRAL TRUTH to be grasped from all of the Spirit's letters to the seven churches, taken together, it is this: We humans look on the outward appearance of things, but God looks upon the heart.

Throughout these letters to the churches, time after time, we are shown that God is not impressed with the things that impress us. This is certainly true when we consider the case of Sardis.

WHAT A "LIVE" CHURCH!

Sardis had a "name," a reputation of being alive (see Rev. 3:1). Her fame was well known throughout the area. This was "the" church to attend. In today's parlance, her parking lot was full every Sunday. The local police were there directing traffic. The community round about could give you directions to the place. The church at Sardis was popular and well attended.

Quite likely the "angel" of this church—the central "bright light" who drew in the crowds—had also become well known and well liked. He hosted a weekly television program as well as producing the yearly Passion Play—not to mention the popular Singing Christmas Tree. Because of his "vision," the church gained its reputation for being alive.

The highlight of the week, of course, was the Sunday morning service. Unless you came early you may have had difficulty finding a seat. Unlike other churches in the area, this church prided itself on its contemporary style of worship, which included short dramas followed by a short well illustrated message built around some "current event."

The "angel" had surrounded himself with some of the brightest and best educated men he could find. There were classes for almost every need, from eating disorders to weight loss. The singles group was the midweek "crown jewel." Here singles of all ages met to fellowship, feast, and discuss how to break free of their past "problems" and get on the road to recovery. Yes, this was the most "dynamic" and alive church around.

And yet....

There was One who held a totally different opinion. The verdict that Jesus, the Lord of the Church, rendered over the church at Sardis was, "You have a name, that you are alive, but you are dead" (Rev. 3:1b).

What was wrong, deep in the spirit of the believers at Sardis? We need to examine this letter with great care, because even the church of Thyatira fared better than Sardis. To begin with, Sardis is the only church that did not receive some commendation—not one word—at the outset. This is alarming, a signal that something is gravely wrong. Jesus immediately moves into condemning her for her lack of completed deeds (see Rev. 3:2).

How could such a popular church fall so short of meeting the Master's approval? Every pastor and spiritual leader should inquire as to exactly what Jesus was looking for. How do we determine what was wrong with this church without injecting our own opinions and bias into the answer?

Fortunately, we have the Spirit's opinion to give us the objective and holy view of things we need in order to correct ourselves.

THE SPIRIT'S-EYE VIEW

Only if we take the Spirit's view will we see things correctly. The first thing we need is a "Spirit's-eye view" of the Church.

When Christ looks upon His Church He is looking for signs that it is, in fact, still His Body, carrying out the functions and works He would accomplish if He were physically present on earth. To Christ, then, the Church is a spiritual organism.

Sad to say, we often look upon any church we are involved in more as an organization. As such, we see that what it needs is a "dynamic" pastor, who is more like a CEO, and an equally "dynamic" staff. Right away, we're off to a very bad start.

There is a basic truth of life that cannot be denied here: The life of a body is derived from its head. In order for a congregation to be part of the true Church and not just "an organization made up of talented Christians," it must be connected to our one true Head, who is Christ Himself. Merely being led by a pastor and elder board, however gifted or knowledgeable or dedicated these people might be, is not enough. The Church at all levels must be connected by the Spirit to Christ, or it will not have the life of the Spirit of Christ flowing into it. Connected to Him we have life—it is inevitable—for Jesus said, "I am come that [you] might have life" (Jn. 10:10b KJV). A dead church is one that has lost its life, or perhaps never had this vital connection to Christ by the Spirit to begin with.

In the case of Sardis, the ministry and operation of the Spirit were missing. That was the problem. Activity was going on everywhere—"programs" abounded—but it was all done by human effort and natural ability. The church was a dynamo of activity but, severed from its Head, its spiritual nerve endings were dead. Without this vital connection it was not being led and empowered by the Spirit.

HOW THIS AFFECTS US

Perhaps another prophetic picture from Scripture, from an earlier time, will help to broaden and deepen our understanding of the problem at Sardis—and how the same problem may plague us.

In the Book of Isaiah, the prophet is given a glimpse of the spiritual malady plaguing the nation of Israel in his day. (See Isaiah 33.) He explains their problem—which is also spiritual deadness—by envisioning Zion as a place of broad rivers and wide canals. Isaiah is seeing "into" the spiritual condition of Israel, for of course Zion represents God's spiritual vision and full purpose for His people.

Zion was also a natural location, situated on the north side of Jerusalem. In fact, it was a natural fortress that made up part of the city. From here, Isaiah explains, the Lord will come to govern His people. From this place, the Spirit of God will flow out, making His will known, empowering His people to do

His will. So Zion, the place from which the Lord Almighty rules, will become "a place of rivers and wide canals." What we see is a place teeming with spiritual empowerment and life in the Spirit!

Isaiah also sees—and this is very important—that Zion will be a place "on which no boat with oars will go, and on which no mighty ship will pass" (Is. 33:21b). Boats with oars are driven by human effort. Their only means of movement is man's natural strength and energy. It is clear that human effort will get us nowhere in the Kingdom of the Spirit!

But continuing, Isaiah compares these useless, man-powered boats to another type of vessel. Of one type he says, "Your tackle hangs slack" (Is. 33:23a). Of the other type he says it is moved along quite powerfully by spreading out "the sail" (see Is. 33:23b). What a descriptive picture we have here of the difference between two types of vessels. One is powered by human effort and the Spirit can move it nowhere; the other is driven along by the wind of the Spirit!

In Sardis, "rowers" were everywhere. This church thrived on human effort. Jesus saw beyond their activity into the heart of a church that knew nothing of the Spirit's empowering. The tragedy was that they had not learned how to hoist the sail and allow the wind to do its work. For the Lord says, "It is not by might nor by power, but by My Spirit" (Zech. 4:6c). The church at Sardis followed the same principle as did the Galatians, who began in the Spirit but ended by seeking to do things in the flesh.

I want to point out one of the grave dangers we each face in studying these letters to the churches. It is easy to read about spiritual deadness and lack of connection to Christ by the Spirit and think, "Yes, the church I attend is dead." Or "My pastor is obviously not connected to the Holy Spirit—so it's no wonder the church is so lifeless." Or, if you're a leader, it's easy to think "These people are dead as doornails." The problem, of course, is always with someone else, isn't it?

It is vitally important that we consider this problem as individual members of the Body. The question is not: How would Jesus classify my church, my pastor, or my congregation? The question must become: How would Jesus classify me—as dead to Him, or alive to Him?

How easy it is for every one of us to lapse into living the Christian life through our own resources, rather than staying in intimate contact with Christ, our divine Head. How easy to live out of our own strengths, rather than in daily dependency upon His Spirit.

As I travel across the nation, I am aware that so few Christians have a daily, personal relationship with Christ by the Spirit. "Give us this day our daily bread" has been replaced with "Give us a good message today through our pastor, and that will sustain us for the week!" The Christian community seeks to live off one or two meetings a week. There is no longer that daily visit to the outflowing river of His presence. As Jeremiah stated, we have "[hewn] for [ourselves] cisterns, broken cisterns that can hold no water" (Jer. 2:13b). We derive our life from television, sports, material goods, and the like. Yes, we send our children to Christian schools, listen to the latest Christian music, attend our local church—but deep within us we have no real hunger for the Spirit, no desire to meditate on God's Word.

Like the believers in Sardis, we may have the appearance of being spiritual—but God sees inside the façade and knows that the empowering life of His Spirit is not in us. All our works have become dead.

NOT JUST DEAD, BUT DEFILED

There is another problem in Sardis, actually, that is made evident by the words of Jesus: "But you have a few people...who have not soiled their garments" (Rev. 3:4a).

This implies that the majority of the church were far from living lives of holiness. The apostle James exhorts us "to keep [ourselves] unspotted from the world" (Jas. 1:27c KJV). But this church—apparently blinded by her own success—had settled into a life of compromise. Quite likely the crowds were still coming. But from the Spirit's diagnosis we realize that nobody gave a second thought to God's opinions—or for that matter, to their own personal relationships with God.

How easily we become attenders of church, rather than abiders in Christ. How quickly program and routine replace relationship. Soon the machinery is running smoothly, and we compare ourselves among ourselves, all the time becoming numb to the life of the Spirit. Before we know it, we are no different from any worldly organization with "a great program" to offer.

King Solomon admonished all people of God with these words, "Let your clothes be white all the time, and let no oil be lacking on your head" (Eccles. 9:8). Surely this is the ideal God intends for His Church. The Greek word for "soil" or "defile" comes from the root word meaning "black." How the Master must grieve when His beloved Bride defiles herself by ignoring His Spirit's voice and guiding hand in order to follow a "successful program."

How does this type of spiritual compromise begin? I believe we have the answer in Revelation 3:2, where Jesus pleaded with His people to "wake up."

The state of spiritual slumber renders us insensitive to what is going on around us. Paul used this same expression in addressing the Romans, when he urged them to "...awaken from sleep..." (Rom. 13:11). He challenged them to "...lay aside the deeds of darkness..." (Rom. 13:12), and then elaborated on what he meant, saying, "Let us behave properly as in the day, not in carousing and drunkenness, not in sexual promiscuity and sensuality....and make no provision for the flesh..." (Rom. 13:13-14).

Jesus said of those in Sardis who had not soiled or defiled their garments that they would "...walk with Me in white..." (Rev. 3:4). The Bible often uses this term "to walk" in describing our pattern of life. Paul, for instance, takes the Ephesian believers back to their former life by stating, "You formerly walked according to the course of this world" (Eph. 2:2a). In contrast, John urges us to "walk, even as [Christ] walked" (1 Jn. 2:6b KJV).

May God grant us today the grace to lay aside the deeds of darkness and walk with Him in white.

HE IS COMING

Jesus warns His people that failure to "wake up" will result in His coming "like a thief in the night" (1 Thess. 5:2c; see also Mt. 24:42-43). What a difference our relationship with Christ makes with regard to His coming!

Those of us who have remained disconnected from our divine Head, Christ, have remained numb to His life and will in us. We have created our own way of compromised Christian living, and we have created our own way—as the slang saying goes—to "do church." We will not be happy to have Him show up suddenly and demand an answer to the question, "What have you done without My direction or approval, in My name?

And why have you pretended to walk in the light, when you still walk in deeds of darkness?"

On the other hand, those with a passion for His presence wait with expectancy and hope, longing for His coming. To them, the sooner He comes, the better. They long to be with the One they have come to love so deeply and passionately.

The writer of Hebrews warns that if we "go on sinning willfully after receiving the knowledge of the truth, there no longer remains a sacrifice for sins, but a terrifying expectation of judgment" (Heb. 10:26-27a). He goes on to say "and if he shrinks back, My soul has no pleasure in him" (Heb. 10:38b). The "drawing back" applies not only to those Hebrew believers who had a tendency to go back to their Jewish ways and practices, but also to those who have allowed their walk to turn back to the things of the world.

CONCLUSION

As you've noted, I have attempted in this chapter especially to apply the directives of the Spirit, written to the church as Sardis, not only to the life of churches today but also to our personal lives as well. That is because spiritual deadness—disconnections from our Head—is a serious and widespread problem among believers. Jesus warned us that in the last days the love of many would wax cold (see Mt. 24:12).

I bring the applications of this chapter down to you, the individual, for a very important reason. There is spiritual wandering and spiritual coolness...and there is clouded spiritual vision due to false teaching and following worldly pleasure. More dangerous than all these is the condition of spiritual deadness—when you can no longer sense the promptings of the life-giving

Spirit. I do not say that no one can find his or her way back from this condition. I do say that no believer should ever want to find out.

In closing, I want to ask you directly: Where would you stand, if today were the day of Christ's return? Would He find you awake or asleep? Would He find your spiritual garment—your soul—pure because your sins have been forsaken and cleansed by His blood, or would you be defiled by sin?

What the Spirit is saying to the Church...what He is saying to each one of us...is this:

"He who overcomes will thus be clothed in white garments; and I will not erase his name from the book of life, and I will confess his name before My Father and before His angels" (Rev. 3:5).

He who has an ear, let him hear what the Spirit says to the churches.

CHAPTER 13

PHILADELPHIA— APPROVED UNTO GOD

ONLY TWO OF THE SEVEN CHURCHES named in Revelation received passing grades.

As we noted, Smyrna was the first to receive highest marks, having endured her fiery trial of persecutions and afflictions. For the believers in Smyrna, Christ was all. Having suffered the loss of everything she remained faithful. My father once said, "You can't say He is all you need until He is all you have." This was the case in Smyrna—all they had left was God, and He was their sufficiency and their "exceeding great reward."

We now come to Philadelphia, the only other church to receive high marks and Christ's seal of approval. As with the other churches, He commences by drawing attention to knowing their deeds or works. The place of works in the Christian's life has become tricky to talk about, and it's a subject we need to examine here.

THE REACTION AGAINST "WORKS"

In reaction to the medieval view of "spiritual works" that was promoted by Catholicism, the Protestant side of the Church has almost universally withdrawn from any emphasis on works. The great revelation of the Reformation was surely that of faith as opposed to works. With this in mind we need to remind ourselves that our salvation is not based on human effort or human merit. "For by grace are ye saved" (Eph. 2:8a KJV).

Once saved, however, we need to understand that "we are His workmanship, created in Christ Jesus for good works..." (Eph. 2:10). Just as our previous life involved us in the works of the flesh, so our new life in Christ should be expressed in good works. It is a true saying that "out of the abundance of the heart the mouth speaks" (Mt. 12:34b NKJV). And it is also true that out of the abundance of the heart the body acts.

The works that we are to perform now are not done in order to gain favor with God. They are done because we have fallen in love with His Son, Jesus, and we love to be directed by His Spirit into works that He wants us to do in His name, on His behalf. To relate this by way of a homey illustration—someone loving the game of golf will not only talk about it but will express his love by also playing the game. Jesus said, "Thou shalt worship the Lord thy God, and Him only shalt thou serve" (Lk. 4:8b KJV). Love is expressed through service.

Paul, who clearly articulated the doctrine of salvation by grace and not by works, nonetheless commended believers for their good works. For instance, he commended the Thessalonians for their "labor of love" (see 1 Thess. 1:3).

THE CRUCIAL DIFFERENCE

The difference between duty and devotion comes down to one factor: motivation. Many believers live lives of fulfilling their God-given duties, but lack the love that should be the motivation force behind such actions. A mother may become tired and weary of the responsibilities of her household, but her love of family is her true motivation to keep going. It is apparent that, for the Philadelphian believers, love was the motivation. Consider.

The saints in Philadelphia were applauded by the Lord for having "kept My Word" (see Rev. 3:8). One can easily pass over the significance of this brief commendation, but what volumes are expressed by such a succinct statement.

Pause for a moment and think of all the commands and admonitions of God's Word. Here are just a few samples: "Love one another" (Jn. 13:34b); "...desire earnestly spiritual gifts" (1 Cor. 14:1a); "Grow in the grace and knowledge of [God]" (2 Pet. 3:18a); "Be kind to one another" (Eph. 4:32a); "...love the Lord your God with all your heart..." (Deut. 6:5); "Beseech the Lord of the harvest to send out laborers into His harvest" (Lk. 10:2b).

In reference to these and all other exhortations, Jesus says these believers have kept His Word. Imagine how different the Church would be if instead of "keeping up with the Joneses" we "kept up with Jesus' words."

Jesus goes further and states that they "have not denied My name" (Rev. 3:8b). This statement goes to the core of what type of believers they really were. Keeping God's Word, while commendable, could come out of merely legalistic or pharisaical hearts. However, when you bring in the honoring of "His name," a new and wonderful quality is added. We realize that these believers were motivated out of their love for Christ Himself.

BLESSED WITH A LITTLE, REWARDED WITH GREAT GAIN

I have purposely skipped over Christ's first commendation of the Church in Philadelphia and left speaking of it till now.

Jesus commends them, saying, "I know that you have a little power" (see Rev. 3:8). The word for "power" here is the Greek word *dunamis*—the same word Jesus used when He said to the disciples, "You will receive power when the Holy Spirit has come upon you..." (Acts 1:8).

The power that the Church at Philadelphia exercises does not have as its source human strength. Rather, it is the power that flows from God Himself. It is supernatural in origin. The word *little* that Jesus uses might seem to be more of a put-down than a commendation. However, this is clearly not the case.

The Philadelphians were a people who had been faithful in "little" things—those common, everyday rubs and buffets that plague us all. In another way, this was no small feat for these Christians because they had used the power of God daily to stand against a constant opposition from those who were in a group Jesus referred to as "the synagogue of satan" (see Rev. 3:9). In short, they had relied steadfastly on God, minute by minute, enduring countless, daily difficulties and apparent persecutions. We know from history that the Roman authorities were enraged by any who failed to swear allegiance to the Empire and to Caesar; and yet here were a people who remained steadfast and refused to deny the name of Jesus. Smyrna was poor and Philadelphia was weak, yet despite their difficult circumstances, both had maintained their love and loyalty to Christ. This all the more enhances what Jesus saw in these glorious saints.

With these things in mind we can glimpse a little better what Jesus had in mind when He said, "...Behold, I have put before you an open door which no one can shut" (Rev. 3:8a). There are two possible explanations for this statement. The first is that it is a promise: He is saying, "Because of your perseverance and loyalty to Me, I will provide you with a guarantee of your entrance into the New Jerusalem." Isaiah the prophet speaks of a day when God is going to prepare a lavish banquet for all His people, when the reproach of His people will be taken away. (See Isaiah 25–26.) Isaiah goes on to speak about the city of God being a strong city with walls and ramparts for security in which the gates or doors will be open to the righteous and the faithful. Perhaps it was this "blessed hope" that Jesus guaranteed to the Philadelphians because He holds the keys of David and has the authority "to open" what "no one will shut."

The other more common explanation is that because of their faithfulness in "little things" they were to be rewarded with greater opportunities, namely, that of having greater influence. The open door was an expression that Paul often used when he spoke about proclaiming the gospel. This promise of "spiritual enlargement" remains today for all those who have stepped out in faith, investing the little that they have been entrusted with, watching as God breaks it and feeds the multitudes through them. The Bible tells us that to each has been given a measure of faith. The Christian life is always progressive; we go from faith to faith and move from victory to victory. How we invest that will determine whether we receive more or not. This church had not retreated in the face of opposition and thus was given a fresh challenge for advancement.

In either case, Jesus says to this church, and to us: "If you sow the little you have, I will see to it personally that you are rewarded with great gain in spirit. And yours will be the increase."

THE SYNAGOGUE OF SATAN

This chapter would not be complete without addressing the "synagogue of Satan" (see Rev. 3:9). This is strong language and would be tantamount to libel if used in some circles today.

The synagogue Jesus refers to is the local community of Jews whose direct purpose was to stand in opposition to the Church, much the way Saul of Tarsus did. They considered it their mission to attack and persecute the Body of Christ in Philadelphia. This was no ordinary resistance but a satanically inspired and energized group of men who were bent on destroying the work of God. When Jesus says they are not Jews (see Rev. 3:9b), He was speaking about their relationship with God. A true Jew, according to Paul, is not one who has been circumcised of the flesh, but of the heart. So Jesus was reminding His Church, "Not all descendants of Abraham are recognized as God's children." Jesus is consistent here with His previous denunciation of the Pharisees, for He had stated, "You are of your father the devil." Why? Because they did the same works as their father.

Jesus promises the Philadelphians that things are going to change and that He will make these "Jews" come and bow before them, acknowledging that God is on their side and that they are the ones greatly loved by God (see Rev. 3:9). Whether this signifies true repentance on the part of these Jews we are not told. Nor do we know if their bowing was genuine or generated.

ARE WE READY?

The Church in America has known little by way of persecution. From what the Bible tells us, however, this is going to change as we approach the last days.

Jesus stated quite emphatically that one of the signs of the last days and His soon coming would be that we would "be hated by all nations because of My name" (see Mt. 24:9). He went on to warn that this would mark the beginning of a time when "many" will fall away.

We would do well to consider these words and begin to prepare ourselves, and the Church, accordingly.

CHAPTER 14

LAODICEA—CAN THESE BONES LIVE?

IF WE TOOK A POLL AS TO WHICH OF THE SEVEN CHURCHES of Revelation was the worst, Laodicea would win by a landslide.

This is not good news because Christian commentators for centuries have associated the condition of the Laodicean believers with the present-day Church. That is to say, many commentators believe that the seven churches represent seven seasons of time, and that Laodicea represents the condition of the Church in the last days prior to the second coming of Christ. It is believed that Laodicea represents the apostate church—the church we are to denounce.

Following this belief, millions of believers have heard the call to "come out from their midst...and do not touch what is unclean..." (2 Cor. 6:17). This has resulted in the burgeoning of tens of thousands of independent churches, as well as hundreds of small house churches. These believers reference the Lord's obvious distaste for an apostate, lukewarm church and do not want to be found among those of whom the Lord says, "I will spit you out of My mouth" (Rev. 3:16b).

A BAD RAP

I am afraid that our assessment of the Laodicean church is exaggerated and off-the-mark. While this church was far from "healthy," it was nevertheless part of the Body of Christ. We must not forget that she was still included in the seven candlesticks among which we see the Spirit of the Lord walking.

I believe there is a very important lesson here for all of us—maybe especially for those of us who make it a special point to say we are witnesses for Christ, Bible believers, and filled with His Spirit, as well.

For years, I have been warned by well-meaning friends not to have anything to do with certain groups of Christians. Nothing hurts me more than to hear this type of reasoning, especially when it comes from so-called mature believers. Nobody naming the name of Christ has the right to dogmatically oppose what Jesus Christ Himself is committed to restoring.

What I am saying is that, before denouncing and judging groups we consider to be lukewarm and maybe even apostate, we would do well to take a minute and ponder what Jesus said about Laodicea. For He referred to these believers as "those whom I love…" (see Rev. 3:19). Here we see expressed the true heart of the Great Shepherd of the sheep.

What a revelation of the heart of God is expressed in the words, "those whom I love." This is the heavenly Hosea, seeking to woo back His erring Bride. This is the Shepherd leaving the ninety and nine to go out in search of the one that has lost its way. Picture Jesus, who wept over Jerusalem, now weeping over His wayward Church, longing to gather them again to Himself.

In His letter to the Laodiceans, we see Jesus revealed as the Bridegroom who knocks on the door of His beloved, longing to be invited in by the ones He has loved with an everlasting love (see Rev. 3:20).

This response—love and longing to see restoration—must be the only reaction of all God's people toward this apostate church. Yet how seldom, if ever, do we hear compassion expressed towards those whose views and beliefs we consider "nonbiblical" and "liberal"? How it grieves me to hear Christian talk-show hosts claiming to have all the answers while forever criticizing some part of the Body of Christ, analyzing and dissecting every jot and tittle of a group's doctrine, and absent of any sense of the compassion and patient love shown by the Shepherd. I love what G. Campbell Morgan says when he writes the following:

> I seldom find men strenuously fighting what they are pleased to call heterodox teaching, and in bitter language denouncing false doctrine, without being more afraid for the men denouncing than for the men denounced. There is an anger against impurity which is impure. There is a zeal for orthodoxy which is most unorthodox. There is a spirit that contends for faith which is in conflict with faith. If men have lost their first love, they will do more harm than good by their defence of the faith. Behind the denunciation of sin there must always be the tenderness of first love if that denunciation is not to become evil in its bitterness. Behind the zeal for truth, there must always be the spaciousness of first love if that zeal is not to become narrowed into hate. There have been men who have become so self-centred in a narrowness that they are pleased to designate as holding the truth, that the very principle for which they contend has been excluded from their life and

service. All zeal for the Master that is not the outcome of love to Him is worthless."[1]

One wonders: How different would the Body of Christ
look if all the self-appointed spiritual diagnosticians actually
"poured in the oil and wine" of healing, rather than recoiling
from this battered, bleeding Body and passing it by on the
other side of the road? Jesus said it is the sick who need a physician (see Mt. 9:12), and for this reason He "went about doing
good and healing all who were oppressed by the devil..." (Acts
10:38b).

As a teacher in the Body of Christ, I often find myself
walking through a "valley of dry bones." Yet I constantly remind
myself that God is able to bring back to life any situation that
appears to be beyond resurrection.

No believer has the right to "give up" on the Church, or
on any part of the Church. If God considers people to be His
true children our work must be what His work is—to
"...strengthen the things that remain" (Rev. 3:2a).

STRENGTHENING WHAT REMAINS

With this attitude in mind we are now able to approach
the task of evaluating what was wrong with God's people in
Laodicea. Once again we are faced with two totally different
viewpoints. One is the outer view of the Church; the other is
the spiritual view of Christ. These two views are diametrically
opposed to each other.

The Laodiceans, we read, consider themselves to be
"wealthy, and [in] need of nothing" (see Rev. 3:17a). We can
well imagine those who attend this church, decked out in high
fashion, very much "in vogue." Christ, on the other hand, sees

her as a blind pauper, filthy, disheveled, and scantily clothed in rags (see Rev. 3:17b).

No doubt in the mind of this local assembly these were some of her finest attributes. How easily we deceive ourselves into thinking that what looks impressive to the world also looks impressive to God. Nothing could be farther from the truth. What man says has no bearing with God. Opinion polls don't matter here. Social status makes no difference, nor does the architecture of the building. God is not impressed with how many personalities attend, or the amount of money given to missions.

PROSPEROUS...AND SELF-SUFFICIENT

It is odd indeed to me—and ironic—that only a couple of decades ago countless believers poured out of old, prosperous, established churches to establish "simple, New Testament churches." We recoiled in horror at the superficiality of worldly wealth, and set out to build a simpler spiritual culture.

And yet...

Today, prosperity has become one of the great yardsticks of spiritual success—even among the "Bible-believing and Spirit-filled" churches. We have, quite simply, recreated the reliance on wealth for which we judged the previous generation. There are more televangelists today than any other period of church history, trying to convince the Body of Christ that the true measure of spiritual maturity is whether you're financially prospering. One almost gets the idea that if you're living on an average income, you're next to being backslidden.

Have we so quickly forgotten what Jesus has to say about this attitude?

Addressing the Pharisees, Jesus states:

"No servant can serve two masters; for either he will hate the one and love the other....You cannot serve God and wealth." Now the Pharisees, who were lovers of money, were listening to all these things....And He said to them, "You are those who justify yourselves in the sight of men, but God know your hearts, for that which is highly esteemed among men is detestable in the sight of God" (Luke 16:13-15).

Here again we have two, divergent opinions expressed—man's view and God's. God does not esteem prosperity the way we do. He sees it as a huge and potentially deadly trap.

This godly view is further exemplified in the incident where Jesus is rudely interrupted by someone in the crowd He is speaking to, asking Him to intervene in a family matter. It seems the man's father had died and his brother refused to share the inheritance with him. Jesus refused to be an arbiter in the situation, but used the circumstances to teach, saying: "...Beware, and be on your guard against every form of greed; for not even when one has an abundance does his life consist of his possessions" (Lk. 12:15).

He proceeds by telling the crowd a parable—the story of the business-savvy rich man who tore down his barns in order replace them with larger ones so he could store the increase in his crops (see Lk. 12:16-20). The one area he failed in, however, was his spiritual preparation. From the outside, men would judge him an excellent workman and brilliant administrator. But Jesus calls him a fool, adding, "So is the man who stores up treasure for himself, and is not rich toward God" (Lk 12:21). Jesus clearly makes a distinction here between the natural and the spiritual when it comes to the matter of "riches."

These and other passages help us to better understand how wealth can so easily become our life. Such was the case with Laodicea. She had become wealthy and gradually deceived herself into thinking that "gain equaled godliness" (see 1 Tim. 6:5). Her life was derived from the abundance of her possessions.

Looking into the mirror of God's Word, in this part of Revelation, my hope is that we will all see how similar the average American church is to our New Testament counterpart. The "life" of most churches revolves around the numerous activities, not to mention their facilities. What was missing in Laodicea was what is missing in so many congregations—"relationship." In Laodicea, we see Christ standing on the outside of a closed door, longing to be invited in (see Rev. 3:20). His Bride, the Church, however, is oblivious to His knocking, choosing rather to find her fulfillment in life from the varied activities she has produced for herself. How tragically the Church today parallels her in almost every way.

Today, more than ever, we have learned how to "excel" without the abiding presence of God in our midst. With our slick marketing techniques, professional staff, and motivational speaking, we are able to operate successfully without God. As someone wisely said, "If the Holy Spirit were to be withdrawn from the earth today, most churches would never realize He was gone."

Perhaps one of the saddest comments regarding this Laodicean church is that they believed they "had need of nothing." This reveals the degree of blindness and deception into which these believers had fallen. There is also incredible pride expressed by these words. The Laodiceans were indeed able to operate alone, not realizing how self-sufficient they had become.

Are we hearing what the Spirit is saying to the Church?

THE LUKEWARM BRIDE

We cannot discuss the Laodicean church without talking about the characteristic for which she is perhaps best known: lukewarmness.

Now under certain circumstances, lukewarmness is better than hot or cold. Take for example a baby's bottle, or living in a moderate climate as opposed to one where there is extreme heat or cold. When it comes to the matter of relationships, however, this is the last thing a lover wants from his beloved. "Lukewarm," "mediocre," "average," and "neutral" are not the types of expressions one wants to hear, especially regarding the one they are about to marry.

Solomon shares what I consider to be the Old Testament counterpart to this story. In his wonderful jewel of a book, Song of Solomon, he tells how at the beginning of their relationship his lover could not get enough of him being her friend and lover. She begins by expressing her longing to be kissed by him, saying, "Your love is better than wine" (Song 1:2b). This bride has found the answer to all her needs in her beloved.

As this story continues we see their relationship deepening over the course of the following chapters. But then in chapter 5 we find the story taking a twist. The bride has gone to sleep for the night when without warning her beloved appears, desiring to be with her. She hears him knocking but fails to respond, thinking to herself, *This is not the best time—I'm clean, comfortable, and tired.* Her lack of responsiveness causes him to be grieved and disappointed, and so he withdraws, leaving her alone.

Eventually, she rouses from sleep and recognizes her mistake. She gets out of bed to open the door, only to discover he's no longer there. Thankfully she comes to her senses and immediately begins searching for him.

The segment of this story that I find so similar to the passage in Revelation is the part where she is in bed. She says to herself, "I've taken off my dress, I've washed my feet," etc. In other words, this is not a dirty bride here, but rather one who knows that she is clean. Her cleanness, though, has given place to complacency. She's clean but comfortable.

How many Christians can be described as clean and comfortable? We're clean—we have shed the old clothes of self-righteousness by acknowledging our need of a Savior. Having experienced the "washing of regeneration," we soon settle down. We are comfortable in the fact that we are now right with God and can testify to His goodness in our lives. We soon become "regular customers" at the house of God and can look back on our former lives as being spiritually dead or cold.

But wait! This is exactly the situation we find in Laodicea. The Laodiceans, though clean and comfortable, had become stagnant in spirit. They had settled into a lifestyle of church attendance, fellowship, and other aspects of "church life." They'd bought into a Christian subculture, just as most have today.

In her book *Leaving Laodicea,* Jeanne Terrell writes:

After evaluating the differences and similarities among the seven churches of Revelation, a conclusion might be drawn that the spiritual problems in Ephesus and Laodicea were much alike. Ephesus was accused of leaving her first love, while Laodicea was reproved for being lukewarm....Abandoning "first love" and being lukewarm are concepts that are often used interchangeably today in the modern church. But there is a marked difference. If they are just two terms for the identical condition, then God is extremely unjust, because He was considerably more harsh with Laodicea than with Ephesus....

The Ephesians were admonished to *"Remember therefore from where you have fallen; repent and do the first works"* (Revelation 2:5)....In the past, they had been in a love relationship with Him. It had been a honeymoon full of that *"first love."* They apparently had ceased to grow in that direction and had even begun to shrink back. However, they did have a formerly healthy relationship to return to....

From all indications, the Laodiceans had no genuine first love to return to. They could not renew a love they never had; theirs had to be created anew. They had no good works to their credit, and seemingly they had never been in close union with the Lord. For the Lord to ask them to return to a former love would have required them to recall their past point of deepest fervency....

The Ephesians could be likened to a woman who falls madly in love and gets married. She has a wonderful, fruitful relationship with her husband, and they have several children. However, after years of household responsibility and familiarity, she slowly loses the passion she once felt for her husband.

The Laodiceans had a different kind of relationship with the Lord. They were like a woman who dates a man but refuses to marry him because she has other priorities she wants to pursue. Instead, she engages in an off-and-on, shallow relationship with him, keeping him on a string but never committing to him.[2]

What was missing was passion—the passion to press on into greater intimacy and knowledge of God. He was no longer their life or love. They knew about Him and could defend their beliefs when challenged. But ask them how much time they spent pursuing Him, and they would likely consider you a religious fanatic. After all, we have grown accustomed to believing that as long as our sins are forgiven, that is all that's necessary.

Here is the problem, as we approach the end of this age. Jesus is not coming back to fulfill the role of some heavenly conductor, walking through the Church checking that we have the correct ticket in order to make the journey we call "the rapture." God forbid. As the Church we must awaken to the reality that the Christian life is more than some divine fire insurance policy. Rather, it is the beginning of an intense, passionate relationship with the living God Himself. The new birth is not the end, but just the very beginning of an ever progressive and exciting relationship with the one and only true and living God.

In terms of natural birth, a baby emerges from a world of darkness into a world of light and thus begins to grow in knowledge and understanding. Likewise, the child of God is taken from a world of spiritual darkness into the glorious light of God's Kingdom. The center of this Kingdom is none other than the King Himself. The new birth not only brings us into this Kingdom, but into the very family of the King. We become not only one of His subjects but one of His children. The King becomes our Father. As our understanding increases we begin to realize what an incredible privilege it is to know the King Himself. Through this glorious relationship we begin to grasp the reality that we were created for something greater than the "world of self." We were created "by Him and for Him" (see Col. 1:16b).

Unless we as Christians grasp this revelation we will not experience the changed perspective that alone can revise our view about ourselves as believers and the lives we are to live. This alone can cure our lukewarmness: We were created to enjoy fellowship with God Himself!

CHRIST IS STILL KNOCKING

The Laodicean church, like the Church today, had lost this living, vital relationship. They no longer derived their satisfaction from intimacy with Christ, but from the fruit of their wealth and comfort. No longer were they satisfied with spending time alone in the presence of the King. Their excitement came from counting the size of the offering or watching the attendance slowly climb until they became the biggest and the best. More time was spent organizing than agonizing in prayer. The intercessors gave way to the intellectuals whose advice was carefully followed. Businessmen now ran the church as they did their own businesses. More time was given to planning than prayer, and so little by little the church changed from a body to a business. People became dispensable and popularity became their goal.

Despite all of this, Christ continues knocking at our door, hoping that we will realize there is no substitute for His presence. Moses refused to settle for the wealth of Canaan with its houses and lands, but rather pleaded with God for His presence (see Ex. 33:13-16). What a tragedy that the Church has failed to grasp the importance of Moses' message and has rather settled for the "milk and honey."

Laodicea failed to understand how close she was to being "expelled." She was blind to her own condition, little realizing that she was being given a final chance for a full and complete recovery, a recovery so remarkable that it included one of the greatest promises made to any of the seven churches: the privilege of sitting and reigning with Christ upon His throne!

Do we realize how greatly we today need to recover our position with Christ?

RECOVERING OUR PLACE IN CHRIST

Before we conclude our study we need to consider the steps given in order to experience, as the Church, the recovery of our true place in Christ.

The first requirement is repentance.

Repentance means to agree with God in His evaluation of my life, regardless of how I or others view myself. It means to turn from my sin and pride, humbly seeking God for His cleansing. Next, we must once again zealously pursue our relationship with Him. How do we do this? It begins by opening our heart again to Him, making Him the focus and center of our lives. Following this we are to spend time with Him in fellowship.

Second, we need to restore our zeal.

Christ seeks for one standard among His people—zealousness. "Therefore be zealous and repent" (Rev. 3:19b). According to the best word studies, *zealous* means "to admire," "to be enthusiastic for," "to strive after," "to have warmth or feeling for." The apostle Paul uses this word when describing how, before his conversion, he went after the early Church, destroying, plundering, and persecuting any and all he could find belonging to "the Way"! This is the type of passion Christ seeks to once again awaken within His people.

The full extent of this zeal can only be appreciated as we consider the term Christ Himself used, in speaking to the Laodiceans: "I wish that you were...hot" (Rev. 3:15b). This word *hot*, when used to describe a liquid, meant to "boil," or when applied to metal, to "glow."

Few of us would be so bold as to declare our love for Christ as white-hot or boiling, and yet to be anything less is to be considered lukewarm.

May God grant us, His Church today, the grace to shake off our complacency and to lay aside our agendas, and press in to know and love Him with fresh love and zeal!

ENDNOTES

1. G. Campbell Morgan, *The Letters of Our Lord* (London: Pickering & Inglis, Ltd., n.d.), p. 27.

2. Jeannie Terrell, *Leaving Laodicea* (Hagerstown, MD: McDougal Publishing, 2001), pp. 41-43.

CHAPTER 15

WARNINGS TO THE CHURCH UNIVERSAL

IT HAS BEEN MY GREAT DESIRE in writing this book that we, today, should hear the voice of the Spirit and what He is saying to the Church. Here, on the threshold of Christ's return, we are in great need; and even more so, the world needs us to be the Church, that more might be saved.

We have covered a great deal of ground as we examined the Spirit's letters to the seven churches in Revelation. I believe it is important here, in closing, to capsulate the urgent essence of these messages.

FOR TODAY...FOR US ALL

Again, I say, it is critical that we keep in mind the universality as well as eternity of truth contained in these seven letters.

By this I mean they are not simply a historic archive, revealing the condition of the early Church. Rather, they are timeless messages for the universal Body of Christ. Moreover, these churches were not randomly selected by some divine lotto. They were specifically chosen by the Spirit of God to reveal to the Church of Christ throughout her earthly pilgrimage the pitfalls and problems to avoid.

To that end, these letters contain a treasure trove of truth for teaching, reproof, correction, and training. As Israel's sins were said to serve as examples for the early Church (today also), so these failures of the early Church serve likewise as a warning to the present-day Body of Christ. What they teach applies both to the corporate body and to us individually. They contain the standards of Christ, against which we will be measured.

It behooves us therefore to pay attention to the Spirit's voice, and to the lessons we need to learn.

BEWARE OF FALLING OUT OF LOVE

The most clear and important message is our call to divine relationship.

That which is of paramount importance to the Lord has nothing to do with size, programs, wealth, or fame. What is most important to Him is that He, alone, is the love of our life. Christ will not tolerate being relegated to anything less than first place.

As Paul made clear to the Colossians, Christ must have "first place in everything" (Col. 1:18b). Any person, program, or passion that replaces Christ is idolatrous in the sight of God. We do well to remember how Peter was desirous of building three tabernacles in his zeal to accommodate Moses and Elijah on the mount of transfiguration; and yet God overshadowed them, leaving only Christ transfigured before them. So we have sought to elevate personalities, denominations, and movements that have replaced Christ from His rightful place of supremacy and centrality.

BEWARE OF "REPLACEMENTS"

Our problem is that this replacement process does not happen suddenly. It takes place gradually.

An example of this is found in the parable of the prodigal son. As this young man matured, he came to the realization that his father had an inheritance set apart for him. From the father's viewpoint this inheritance was to be of great blessing to his son. Its advantages were enormous. It had the means of establishing the son for the rest of his life. The father had worked to provide for his sons. He had selflessly set aside his own wealth in order to bless his sons. It was never the purpose of the father to withhold from his sons that which was in their best interests. The son, on the other hand, began to desire more. He was far from satisfied with his present condition and knew that his father wanted to bless him. His older brother, unfortunately, was satisfied to remain impoverished and had no desire to partake of the father's wealth.

There are some striking similarities between this story and many within the Father's house today. We have seen a young generation arise that has not been satisfied with the older generation's example of Christianity. This younger generation has heard that the Father has an inheritance reserved and ready for the asking. This inheritance comprises the Father's wealth—his wealth of wisdom, power, gifts, authority. Failing to see their brothers pursuing these things, they have begun to implore the Father that he release to them His wealth—their inheritance.

Having received the inheritance, the son's focus shifted from seeking more from his father to reveling in his newfound inheritance. The inheritance then became the object of his desire and the love of his life. Slowly his newfound inheritance drew him away from his relationship with his father and he began to derive his pleasure from the gift that his father gave him.

This story illustrates one of our greatest dangers in the Church today. We focus on our great blessings, and in time our love for our blessings replaces our love for God. Whatever term we use to describe our inheritance—whether it be anointing, gifts, authority, or calling—none of these blessings was ever meant to become a substitute for the greatest of all inheritances—Christ.

BEWARE OF COMPROMISE

Yet another clear message we receive is that Christ will not tolerate any teaching or doctrine that leads to compromise with regard to His standard of holiness.

God is holy and has purposed before the foundation of the world that "we would be holy and blameless before Him" (Eph. 1:4b). Once again we need to see that this is both a universal and eternal truth and so applies to the universal Church and also the twentieth-century Church.

The very thought of harboring a Jezebel or Balaam in our midst would cause most believers to recoil. And yet their teachings continue unabated in our midst today. The same spirit of compromise pervades. Christians get drunk, get high, and get divorced, as they freely mingle with the world and adopt its attitudes and its ways. Mass culture has gradually dulled our sensitivity to God's standards of morality and purity. Many Christians know far more about Hollywood personalities than they do of biblical ones. They stumble to recite the Books of the Bible but have no problem naming the various teams in the NFL or NBA.

The love of the world is deeply rooted in the Western Church, and attempts to challenge it are most often met with cries of legalism.

As we noted earlier, we have repackaged God so as to make Him "user friendly." The God who is jealous for His holiness has been elbowed aside by the new happy face model and always smiles approvingly at whatever we say or do. Here again these teachings don't appear overnight but gradually. Peter warns us that false teachers will creep in secretly, the end result being that they deny the Master who bought them (see 2 Pet. 2:1) and replace Him with other things.

BEWARE THE DOWNWARD SPIRAL

In several letters to the churches, we saw what might be termed "the downward spiral."

First comes the failure to acknowledge some aspect of His lordship over our lives. We compromise our standard of holiness. Other priorities and values, and love for the world itself, replaces Him. This then leads to everyone doing what is right in his own eyes. God's call to "separate" ourselves unto Him is denied. We then fall prey to the world's pressure towards "toleration." To be tolerant is defined: "to recognize and respect the rights, opinions, and practices of others." This sounds good, but as time passes we progress from toleration to cooperation, freely working together toward a common goal.

The final stage of this downward spiral is that of "adoption," which the dictionary defines as "to take and follow a course of action, to take on or assume, to choose as a standard."

From our position in Christ—where we were adopted into God's own family—the Church has slidden downward. Today the message of holiness falls on deaf ears. We no longer pride ourselves as a "peculiar people," but desire rather to be a "popular people." The call to come out from among them and be separate is met with stiff resistance from God's people. Little do we realize how we have become conformed to this world. Our whole lives have absorbed the world's influence, with its philosophy, practices, and policies. At the bottom of the spiral, we find ourselves adopting the ways of the world.

BEWARE LEST YOUR LIGHT GO OUT

If you recall the opening chapters of this book, you will remember what Christ was doing as His Spirit walked among the seven lamps. He was trimming the wicks, refilling them with oil, lest their lights go out, rendering His churches useless and plunging the world into spiritual darkness.

Today, the world takes little notice of us—except to point out our gross compromises, failures, and the quirkiness of our little subculture. We fail to present them with a radically different choice, because we have desired to be just like them. Yes, Balaam and Jezebel are alive and well and flourishing among us.

CONCLUSION

Brothers and sisters in Christ, today the Spirit is calling us once again to "come out from their midst and be separate" (2 Cor. 6:17a).

CHAPTER 16

TO THE BRIDE

As WE COME TO THE END of this study, I want to leave you with a vision of what the Church, the Bride of Christ, can become. If we heed the voice, the warnings, and the ministrations of the Spirit, we can become the pure and spotless Bride of Christ we are called to be.

For that, we turn to the end of John's great vision, where we find one of the seven angels speaking to John with these words: "Come here, I will show you the bride, the wife of the Lamb" (see Rev. 21:9b).

Let us, in closing, consider the beauty of the Bride of Christ, as He longs to see her.

LONGING FOR INTIMACY WITH HIM

Throughout the whole of Scripture, the relationship of Christ with His Church is likened unto the marriage relationship. This relationship was prefigured from the very beginning.

Starting in Genesis we see how from the physical side of Adam God created for him a bride and presented him with Eve. So likewise, from the side of the last Adam, God brought forth the Church, which He will one day present to His Son as a glorious Bride.

As the Old Testament unfolds, the story of Hosea and Gomer beautifully illustrates the tender, compassionate, and patient character of God towards His people Israel—for whom He grieves just as Hosea grieves for his wayward bride.

Paul, dealing with the subject of marriage in the New Testament, says, "This mystery is great; but I am speaking with reference to Christ and the church" (Eph. 5:32). Addressing the Corinthians he tells them of his desire: "For I betrothed you to one husband, so that to Christ I might present you as a pure virgin" (2 Cor. 11:2b).

These and other passages reveal the type of relationship Christ is longing to have with us. There is no more intimate relationship than that of a husband and wife. There is no friendship that surpasses it. "They shall become one flesh" (Gen. 2:24b) describes a union like no other.

One of the great beauties of a healthy, intimate marriage is that the longer the relationship goes on, the greater the depth of intimacy we may experience with one another. Just the other day my own pastor, David Hickey, was sharing how he and his wife were alone together for several days. He related how exciting those days were, then added, "I didn't know where I ended and she began"—such was the oneness they had together.

This is the way Christ longs to see us—longing for intimacy with Him.

HEALTHY AND FRUITFUL

Women very often typify the Bride of Christ.

Take, for example, women in the Scriptures who were unhealthy or barren. Barrenness typifies the condition of the Church apart from the indwelling presence of God. Jesus said just as the branch cannot bring forth fruit unless it abides in the vine, so neither can we apart from Christ.

Mark's Gospel tells the story of a woman whom Jesus healed after 12 years of affliction (see Mk. 5:25-34). As I've studied this story, I've come to understand how many similarities there are between what this woman went through in the natural to the spiritual counterpart in the Church. I believe this story has prophetic significance for the Church today.

The first thing we notice about this woman was *she was dying*. She was continually losing blood and her very life was slowly ebbing away. Day after day she was growing weaker and weaker. The only strength she had left was spent in looking after her own needs. As we've seen, the similarities with the Church are obvious. We have become anemic.

What do I mean by *anemic*?

I ask: Where is our spiritual power? No longer can we declare, "Silver and gold have I none; but such as I have give I thee: In the name of Jesus Christ...rise up and walk" (Acts 3:6 KJV). The early Church turned the world upside down, raised the dead, cleansed the lepers, and cast out demons. And all this was accomplished by unlettered men who never sat in a seminary, never sent out a newsletter, and had no "covenant partners" to guarantee their support. They simply cast themselves upon God and drew upon His power for their physical and spiritual needs.

Second, we see that the woman with the issue of blood was *despised*. The normal menstrual cycle according to the law classified a woman as unclean and untouchable. Whatever she touched became unclean; likewise, wherever she sat became defiled. Anyone touching her was to be unclean for seven days. Who in their right mind would want to hang around a woman like this? If she had a husband he had the right, according to the law, to leave her if he chose. Otherwise they could have no intimacy together. To touch her would render you unclean. No doubt the very mention of her name was offensive to many, and people would run to avoid making contact with her. She was never invited into a home, never held or cherished. Nothing about her was attractive. She had long ago lost her reputation.

It's very apparent that much of what we know about this woman in the natural applies to the Church today. Mention the Church to the average man on the street and he is likely to tell you some horror story and provide a dozen reasons why he's no longer interested in being "with her." The Church today is far from being clean, even in the eyes of the world. Today, the world hears only of the never-ending failures of pastors, church splits, misappropriation of funds, and other abuses. We have become diseased.

And yet, Christ sees us as we can be—if we repent and return to Him—and that is healthy and fruitful.

The third thing we see in this woman was that she was *discouraged.* Any prolonged, persistent, chronic problem leads eventually to discouragement. For 12 years she had suffered and yet not because she hadn't sought for an answer—she had. The passage reveals that she had sought for help over and over again. She had not only suffered physically from being prodded and poked by every so-called expert, but also financially.

The end result, according to the text, was that she had "endured much" and had "grown worse." Every new physician she saw promised her some cure. She went expecting, longing to be delivered, only to find they gladly accepted her money but could do nothing to help. Due to her condition she was forced to seek help outside of the Jewish community.

No doctor wanted to be unclean for a week and so she turned to the world for help.

Does all this sound familiar? There is widespread discouragement throughout the Body of Christ. We have tried everything looking for answers to our "illness." The years roll by and we are still as weak as ever. We've even turned to the world for help and are no better for it—if anything we too have "grown worse." According to a recent survey, 70 percent of today's pastors would leave the ministry if they had another way to support themselves and their families. Seventy percent of all pastors constantly experience depression. In the last decade a significant number of pastors' wives have walked away from their marriages and even children, unable to cope with the pressure of the ministry.

Next we see that she was *distracted.* This woman should have been busy raising a family. Instead of being fruitful she had become self-absorbed, focusing on her own needs and problems, having little time for anything else. No longer could she meet the needs of those round about her. Instead she was running from one physician to the next trying to find a cure for her own troubles.

How much time, money, and energy does the average church or believer spend on seeking to meet the needs of those around them? We too have become distracted with ourselves and our own needs. We have lost sight of our calling. Most of our resources are used to alleviate our own ailments. I realize that there are some exceptions, but generally speaking, this is not an unfair assessment.

If there is one positive note in the story so far it has to be that *she was desperate.* She refused to take no for an answer. We don't find her going home to die. Something within her kept her going. Perhaps it was the testimonials of friends or neighbors who had "discovered" a new cure being advocated by the new doctor in town. Again she made her appointment, hoping this time what had worked for others would also satisfy her needs as well. Finally her day arrived. She couldn't wait. After all, she had had such great references from friends and family. But after being subjected to the usual battery of tests, she came away poorer, yes, not just physically but also financially. The Bible descriptively states, "She...was not helped at all" (Mk. 5:26c).

Like the woman in this story I, too, have observed over the past 39 years of ministry the Church running from seminar to seminar, from expert to expert, hoping that somehow they might discover the "magic potion" that would raise them from the bed of sickness. I've watched as smaller nations have spent thousands flying in some overseas speaker for a national conference in hopes of discovering his secrets to success. It is not a result of not trying but that of sheer and mounting desperation. Someone has to have the answer.

Finally, we discover that she was *deceived*—deceived into thinking that man had the answer to her situation. Let's face it, these men were experts in medicine—doctors, if you like. Unfortunately, they didn't have the power to set her free and rather than lightening her load, they increased it by making things worse. There she was—depleted physically, emotionally, socially, spiritually, and also financially. Her condition had cut her off from the house of God. Her friends who were fading fast could not touch her for fear of becoming unclean. She might as well have been a leper. Now after 12 years of searching for a cure, she was at her wits' end. The Bible said she "had spent all that she had..." (Mk. 5:26b).

Not unlike this woman, the Church has been deceived into thinking that man holds the answer to her needs. I've observed over the years the Church making her rounds of the doctors' offices seeking help. Allow me to introduce you to a few of them—although I'm sure you've sat in their offices yourself at sometime or another.

Let's begin with Dr. Self-Help. His diagnosis reveals that you have a self-image problem, low self-esteem—perhaps a failure mentality. He suggests that you make an appointment with his partner, Dr. Confession. This expert picks up from where the previous doctor ended, prescribing a series of "verses" that if taken daily will do wonders for the immune system, restoring it back to health. You have to admit that this is a great improvement from "I think I can, I think I can, I think I can." After weeks or months of treatments you still feel as though something is wrong or missing. It's then that you hear about Dr. Inner Healing. This doctor, we are told, looks beyond the present symptoms and looks to the root of the problem. Sure enough, he finds some long forgotten "hurt" that has caused the tree to grow crooked. Now finally you are on the right track. It has nothing to do with you but rather the way you were raised. You're feeling better already—after all, it's not your fault.

Dr. Inner Healing in his loving, compassionate way suggests that just to be sure you've covered all the bases you should see his associate, Dr. Generational Sins. His expertise, you are told, goes beyond "your" problems and deals with your "family tree." Well now that he mentions it you can think of several serious issues without even beginning to delve into the murky waters of the past. First there is your mother and her controlling spirit, then your father's past association with the Masons—not to mention your uncle's alcoholic problems and your grandmother's addiction to gambling. Well, after numerous visits to Dr. Generational Sins, you begin to grasp that your problems are not really yours. "My father ate sour grapes" and it caused "my teeth to be set on edge."

Just like this woman the Church has made the rounds from one wind of doctrine to the next. The list is almost endless. Dr. Faith had his day in the sun but was soon replaced by Dr. Prosperity. Some recent additions to the medical staff include Dr. Prophetic and his up and coming friend, Dr. Apostolic. Rumor has it that Dr. Apostolic has the cure for almost all our "ills." He is presently receiving almost unprecedented press and appearing at conferences all over the place.

We need to keep in mind that the reason these doctors stay in business is that they do have the occasional "miracle." Not everything they prescribe is wrong. The problem is that most of these doctors have tunnel vision, and think that their particular cure holds the answer to every "sickness."

The Bible tells us this woman "suffered much." She had made the rounds, and instead of being helped, had grown worse. "And hearing about Jesus," she was *delivered and delighted*. Finally after 12 long years of suffering when she had spent all she had, she heard about Jesus. Church, it's time we heard about Jesus again.

The Lord longs for His Bride to become healthy and fruitful, to be delivered of her soul-sicknesses and delighted in Him again.

DEAR CHURCH...

We have spent far too long pursuing other sources of life and need to return to Christ Himself. We have seen in this study of the seven churches that there is no substitute for the presence of God.

Now it is time for us to return to our first love, the Great Physician Himself. He alone has the answers to all our needs. He has come that we might have life in all its abundance. We need to seek Him as this woman did, pressing through the obstacles until we touch Him afresh.

How easily we turn aside, as Jeremiah said: "My people have committed two evils: They have forsaken Me, the fountain [source] of living waters, to hew for themselves cisterns, broken cisterns that can hold no water" (Jer. 2:13). These broken cisterns can be anything we substitute in place of Christ Himself. They can be ministry gifts, congregations, reputations. God is never to become simply a means to an end. He is the end.

GOD IS OUR ALL IN ALL

Paul counted all else but Christ as rubbish (see Phil. 3:8). David said, "Besides You, I desire nothing on earth" (Ps. 73:25b). David had climbed to the pinnacle of position and power and yet was not satisfied.

Like the prodigal we need to arise and forsake everything that we thought could satisfy, return to the Father's house, and fall into the arms of the Father again. Charles Stanley conveys my thought clearer than I can when he writes:

> I believe with all my heart that it is impossible to be both goal-oriented and God-oriented at the same time. One orientation will always take precedence over the other...when our desire to achieve takes the lead several things happen in our relationship with God. He becomes a means to an end rather than the end. We tend to use God rather than worship Him.

We find ourselves seeking information about Him rather than transformation by Him.[1]

Just like the woman whose life was ebbing away we need to reach out and take hold of the only source of life—Christ Himself. He and He alone is the answer to all our needs and desires.

Church, let us respond to His invitation, "If any man thirst, let him come unto Me, and drink..." (Jn. 7:37b KJV).

ENDNOTE

1. Charles Stanley, *A Touch of His Freedom* (Grand Rapids, MI: Zondervan Publishers, 1991), p.152.

UNRAVELING THE COMPLEXITIES OF SPIRITUAL WARFARE

OVER THE COURSE OF THE PAST COUPLE OF DECADES the Church has become increasingly aware of the spiritual battle she is facing. There is an all-out war between the Church and the diabolical strategies of hell. Satan knows that his time is short and has therefore turned up the heat. Everywhere we turn we see the enemy's web of deception being woven in order to lure in the ignorant and innocent. I recently read an article in *Time* magazine dealing with the incredible rise of interest in yoga here in the United States. What was alarming about the article was that it dealt with the growing spread of yoga for children. All across America children as young as three are taught how to "go on a journey" to visit a garden or zoo, to fly like a bird, etc.

All this, according to their teachers, helps to teach children self-esteem and self-expression. Added to this we have the phenomenal success of the Harry Potter empire. Some 48 million books have already been sold and a major motion picture has pulled in millions of dollars. This world of magic, sorcery, and witchcraft has captured the minds, imaginations, and hearts of the youth of this generation like nothing else before it. A recent survey among young teenage girls revealed that their greatest interest was witchcraft—not money, popularity, boys, education, or fashion. The list is endless. The devil is serious about his mission of establishing his kingdom in the hearts of this generation. Yes, we are at war—but how do we enforce the victory that is already ours through Calvary?

One of the strategies of war is to deploy decoys in various places. These decoys appear as legitimate weaponry by the opposing side, and therefore become targets of attack. This not only weakens their fighting power but also wastes valuable time and reserves. I'm convinced that the Church today has been drawn aside by the clever ploy of the enemy in his effective use of decoys.

In our consideration of the Jezebel teaching we saw how "her children" had become engrossed in the "deep things of satan." I believe in our sincere desire to understand the enemy's devices, we too have become enmeshed in her depths as well as misled by her decoys.

On a recent trip to Mexico where I was teaching at a Bible school, the school director showed me a video of a group of intercessors who had taken the arduous task of scaling one of the high mountains in Nepal, I believe. This sincere and adventuresome group had established a base camp while others in the party had forged ahead up beyond the limits of plants and trees and into the bleak snow and ice-covered rocks close to the summit. It was here they discovered a large ledge of rock protruding out from the mountain under which had formed a huge stalagmite of ice. Upon discovering this unique formation it was determined that here was the throne of some major principality. As the group prayed and watched, one of the team took his ice axe and proceeded to hack in pieces this stalagmite, thereby destroying this principality within.

It is this type of warfare that has led the Church off course. This is one of many decoys that the enemy has perpetuated within the Church that has absorbed time, effort, and also valuable resources. The name given to this type of warfare would be classified under the term "high places." The Old Testament belief that high places were bastions of power devoted to various gods has become widely accepted within the Body of Christ. We have accepted the natural majesty of mountains as being applicable to where demon strongholds are found today. While all error contains a margin of truth, let's not allow the enemy to con us into the belief that demons are only interested in high places. Demons are far more interested in possessing people than places. We have no biblical record of Jesus ever casting a demon out of a high place, but dozens of incidents of Him taking authority over demons dwelling in individuals. The New Testament, which contains "everything pertaining to life and godliness," is silent when it comes to this type of warfare.

Another decoy is spiritual mapping. This recent "invention" was unknown to the saints of the past. If the Church would simply learn to pray fervently to God, I'm convinced we would see untold victories. Instead we dissipate time and energy exploring the murky waters of our city's or nation's past in the hope of uncovering some ancient "landing strip" that provided access to our present problems. This type of "theology" provides the enemy with an endless list of "sites" yet to be discovered by God's people.

Still another increasingly popular trend in spiritual warfare circles is the whole arena of reconciliation. This growing
belief seeks to right the wrongs of the past generations' sins.
Once again this provides an unending resource for the enemy
to sidetrack us in. Much of this teaching is rooted in a few Old
Testament passages. What we need to understand concerning
this type of ministry is that God held Israel accountable for
their actions because they and they alone were His sole repre-
sentatives in the world. We have no record of God holding
other nations to this same standard. Israel never became proxy
for the sins of another nation, but simply their own. Likewise,
it is wrong to assume that God's people today bear the responsibility of guilt for sins committed by America, Britain, or any
other godless nation. The Church is a nation alone, having her
unique and privileged place as not being included among the
other nations. Why then are we forever seeking to right the
wrongs of those we are not classified among? Where I can
wholeheartedly give my approval to reconciliation is within the
Church. If we would seek to right these wrongs, I believe we
would begin to experience an unprecedented move of God's
blessing. I was recently attending a four-day conference which
included a number of other churches. Each night, a different
congregation's worship team led the first part of one of the
four evening sessions. One evening the pastor of one of the
worship teams publicly apologized to the host pastor and his
congregation for some past problems between their two
churches. I watched as the two senior pastors prayed and em-
braced one another and felt God's smile of approval on what
was taking place.

In the previous chapter we looked at the story of the
woman with the issue of blood and the fact that she had sought

help from numerous physicians. As I mentioned, the reason these physicians stayed in business was because they must have received some testimonials from their patients. Likewise, with these teachings on spiritual warfare, there are some testimonies of valid results being obtained. However, the true key is obedience to the leading of the Holy Spirit, not simply taking someone else's method and expecting the same results.

One of the great needs in the Church is that we return to the simplicity of God's Word. We have complicated things to the point that the average believer stands confused. It's time we took a fresh look at this whole area of teaching regarding spiritual warfare.

My father was a real man of prayer. Prayer was his life. He would spend hours a day on his face before God. I seldom remember my father talking very much about spiritual warfare. His view of God was so much greater than his view of the devil. He didn't concern himself with the devil because his God was greater than all the forces of darkness. The verses I do recall hearing my father talk about are Psalm 81:13-14: "Oh, that My people would listen to Me, that Israel would walk in My ways! I would quickly subdue their enemies and turn My hand against their adversaries." My father would then comment, "As long as Israel was in a right relationship with God the enemy was never a problem." God's problem in the Old Testament was never with the Amorites, Hittites, or Jebusites. God's problem was always with His people Israel. If Israel walked in obedience to God and His ways, God consistently took care of their enemies—regardless of the odds against them either numerically or militarily. Take, for example, the promise of Deuteronomy 20:1-4:

> When you go out to battle against your enemies and see
> horses and chariots and people more numerous than you,

do not be afraid of them; for the Lord your God, who brought you up from the land of Egypt, is with you. When you are approaching the battle, the priest shall come near and speak to the people. He shall say to them, "Hear, O Israel, you are approaching the battle against your enemies today. Do not be fainthearted. Do not be afraid, or panic, or tremble before them, for the Lord your God is the one who goes with you, to fight for you against your enemies, to save you."

What an incredible promise! I especially like the phrase "to fight for you." The Church has become so devil conscious that we have forgotten that "If God is for us, who is against us?" (Rom. 8:31b)

There is only one reason why we suffer defeat at the hands of the enemy and that is because of sin. There are numerous Scriptures to support this. Let's take a look at some. Following Israel's first victory upon entering the land of Canaan where they saw the walls of Jericho flattened, they advanced toward the little town of Ai. Elated over Jericho, they considered Ai an easy target and so sent only two or three thousand men, saying "for they are few" (see Josh. 7). The men of Ai fought against them and destroyed some 36 men, causing the rest to flee for their lives. Joshua, defeated and discouraged, falls down before God, complaining that God allowed them to be delivered into the hands of their enemies. God speaks to Joshua, telling him to "get up" and asked, "Why is it that you have fallen on your face?" Then God reveals the reason why Israel was defeated. "Israel has sinned. Therefore the sons of Israel cannot stand before their enemies."

The reason Israel suffered defeat had nothing to do with the size or strength of the enemy—that was immaterial. It was solely due to Israel's sin of disobedience in failing to keep God's word. Joshua learned a valuable lesson that day, which stood him in good stead. We are told that Joshua "took all that land....There was not a city which made peace with the sons of Israel...they took them all in battle" (Josh 11:16,19). Joshua, more than any other leader in the Word of God, typifies the Christian's role of advancing God's purpose. He is the foremost warrior and conqueror. The Bible says "Joshua was old, advanced in years...Joshua called for all Israel" (see Josh. 23:1b-2a). He then begins to remind Israel of God's faithfulness.

> *And you have seen all that the Lord your God has done to all these nations because of you, for the Lord your God is He who has been fighting for you....For the Lord has driven out great and strong nations from before you; and as for you, no man has stood before you to this day. One of your men puts to flight a thousand, for the Lord your God is He who fights for you, just as He promised you. So take diligent heed to yourselves to love the Lord your God. For if you ever go back...know with certainty that the Lord your God will not continue to drive these nations out from before you* (23:3,9-13a).

In these verses we have all that is necessary in understanding the important issue regarding spiritual warfare—loving obedience to God and His Word. That places God on your side and victory is assured. There is nothing in these passages concerning spiritual mapping, etc. In fact, it was when Israel decided to go and assess the land that they got into serious trouble. They sent in ten spies, even though God had given them His word that they could possess the land. The spies "mapped out" the land and discovered walled cities and giants.

Having gathered this information, they used it to provoke fear and unbelief in the people, which in turn set them back for 40 years. This was never a part of God's intention. Notice these words in Deuteronomy 1:21-22a. Moses is speaking: " 'See, the Lord your God has placed the land before you; go up, take possession, as the Lord, the God of your fathers, has spoken to you. Do not fear or be dismayed.' Then all of you approached me and said, 'Let us send men before us, that they may search out [map out] the land for us...' " Unfortunately Moses agrees with this "good idea"; however, it was not a God idea.

Repeated throughout the Word, God promises His people that He will fight on their behalf, provided that they walk in obedience to His Word. We have sidestepped the importance of this one simple and yet imperative truth and replaced it with a vast spectrum of complex "solutions." Unfortunately, the average believer in his biblical insecurity has become caught up in new "winds of doctrine," believing that these so-called experts have discovered some lost revelation that holds the key to spiritual victory.

In reading some of the "new" theories, I've noticed that these experts seldom if ever give a satisfactory biblical foundation for their beliefs. They usually quote one another to support their "teachings." There appears to be greater fraternization than true revelation.

Only today I received an e-mail from some intercessors requesting prayer for their assignment, which included a trip to Washington, D.C. Here is part of the report: "Already there seem to be divine connections coming into place to assist us in getting into the right locations to pray." I was always taught that the right location was in your closet on your face before God. Now the right location seems to be geographical, not spiritual.

Am I missing something? Is there some new revelation concerning prayer that I have missed for the past 39 years? Does God really require me to go to "a place" in order to be effective? Isn't the finished work of Calvary all I need to receive answers to prayer? Why all of a sudden is spiritual warfare so complex?

One of the greatest classics on intercession is Reese Howells' *Intercessor* (Christian Literature Crusade). During the Second World War, Reese Howells, along with other unknown intercessors, turned what many considered an inevitable victory for Germany into defeat. There on his face before God, this spiritual giant saw the great and mighty German army brought to its knees. Today we would advise these intercessors to travel to Germany, "the place" where the problem is located, in order to be successful. Show me a single verse of Scripture, especially in the New Testament, where there is even the faintest hint of such teaching, let alone a major doctrinal emphasis.

I believe we are bordering on serious error if we continue along these lines. We have fabricated a whole new approach to spiritual warfare that I see wholly without any scriptural merits whatsoever. We are in grave danger of becoming occultish in our methods. I recently heard of a well-known group of intercessors who traveled to the four corners of their state in order to partake of communion. Following the communion service, they buried the emblems in the ground to act as some sort of barrier, thereby prohibiting the enemy access into their state. This method may work for keeping termites out of your house, but is fruitless in keeping the enemy out of your state. This is akin to keeping a rabbit foot in your pocket, believing that it holds some mystical power to protect you from harm. Wouldn't logic also cause us to believe that if "spirits" can't invade our state because of this practice, then spirits already in the state could not leave it?

Still another popular method of "warfare" is the whole area of pageantry. This includes banners, streamers, flags, etc. Intercessory groups spend hundreds of hours painstakingly designing and creating these beautiful works of art. While these banners may add some life to the walls of their church buildings, they are powerless as weapons of war. We have attributed to these flags and banners supernatural power, believing that when they are waved the enemy trembles. Now tell me, does this differ from the poor ignorant heathen who cuts down a tree from the jungle and carves himself a "god," then bows before it in the hope that it will protect him and his family from evil?

When questioned concerning these practices, most have no answers—at least give no biblical support. Others look at you in disbelief, feeling sorry for the fact that you can't grasp the "revelation" that they have received on these things. These "revelations" transcend the Word of God, but have become real to those who believe them. This to me is what John refers to as "the deep things of satan."

I sometimes feel like Jude, earnestly "contend[ing] for the faith which was once for all handed down to the saints" (Jude 3b). My burden is to restore intercession back into the hands of the "common people." The thousands of praying men and women who have faithfully raised their voices to the throne of God, crying out for lost souls to be saved, cities to be awakened by revival, and nations to turn from the power of satan to God. Possibly the worst thing to happen to the teaching of intercession was when someone gave it the title of ministry or gifts of intercession. This took intercession "out of the closet" and onto the platform. Here in the limelight of popularity this simple sacred calling was forced to sharpen its image in order to appeal to the masses. New and more intriguing methods began to scratch the itch of those looking for excitement. Plain old-fashioned prayer was out, replaced by an ever increasing array of new methods and ways. Those wanting to be known as the "leaders" in this newly discovered "market" continue to receive new revelations. This assures them of their rankings as well as providing them with support necessary to keep churning out something new.

May God open our eyes afresh to the value of "the effective prayer of a righteous man can accomplish much" (Jas. 5:16b). A right heart before God is all that is necessary for answered prayer. The enemy has succeeded in diverting the Church's attention away from being internally right with God to being externally focused. Without exception every new facet of teaching with regards to spiritual warfare deals with something external—being in the right place, anointing some object, lifting a banner, mapping some site, blowing the shofar, wearing a prayer shawl, researching an area, walking some ancient path, reconciling with some "native," etc., etc. All these activities give one the sense of accomplishment and satisfaction. It becomes a "work" rather than "the prayer of faith." This is turn leads to the gradual belief that our methods hold a power of their own—a form of transubstantiation, if you will. For instance, many people falsely assume that lifting a banner or blowing the shofar or even wearing a "Jewish" prayer shawl actually are a means of empowerment when it comes to prayer. It was for this reason the Book of Hebrews was written—to appeal to those who desired to return to their Jewish roots with its rich traditions and symbolism. We need to recognize that these are but shadows, the substance of which is Christ.

Intercessors, it's time to return to the closet and shut the door. Shutting the door is more than closing an opening, but also has to do with avoiding things that can easily distract us from praying and waiting for God. After all, "He who comes to God must believe that He is and that He is a rewarder of those who [diligently] seek Him" (Heb. 11:6b).

Also
by David Ravenhill

THEY DRANK FROM THE RIVER AND DIED IN THE WILDERNESS

by David Ravenhill

Move from the place of *privilege* to the place of *purpose*, from the people of God *among* the nations, to the priests of God *to* the nations. The river is not the goal! It's the gate! Cross and enter—God's promises are in the promised land! Wildness is in the wilderness! The wilderness is only the *bridge* between slavery and sonship—Egypt and Canaan. Don't die en route!

ISBN 0-7684-2038-5

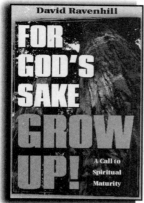

FOR GOD'S SAKE GROW UP!

by David Ravenhill

It's time to grow up...so that we can fulfill God's purposes for us and for our generation! For too long we've been spiritual children clinging to our mother's leg, refusing to go to school on the first day. It's time to put away childish things and mature in the things of God—there is a world that needs to be won to Christ!

ISBN 1-56043-299-3

For those interested in contacting the author for speaking engagements write to:

David Ravenhill
Spikenard Ministries Ltd.
16858 Hwy 110 North
Lindale, TX   75771

Or call:
903-882-3942

Or FAX:
903-882-3740

Available at your local Christian bookstore.

For more information and sample chapters, visit www.destinyimage.com